Let the Sun Shine In

Other Books by Scott Miller

From Assassins to West Side Story:
The Director's Guide to Musical Theatre

Deconstructing Harold Hill:
The Insider's Guide to Musical Theatre

Rebels with Applause:
Broadway's Groundbreaking Musicals

In the Blood
a novel

Let the Sun Shine In

The Genius of Hair

Scott Miller

HEINEMANN ■ Portsmouth, NH

Heinemann
A division of Reed Elsevier Inc.
361 Hanover Street
Portsmouth, NH 03801–3912
www.heinemanndrama.com

Offices and agents throughout the world

Library of Congress Cataloging-in-Publication Data
Miller, Scott, 1964–
   Let the sun shine in : the genius of Hair / Scott Miller.
    p. cm.
   ISBN 0-325-00556-7 (alk. paper)
   1. MacDermot, Galt. Hair.   I. Title.

ML410.M117M54 2003
782.1'4166—dc21   2003001070

Editor: Lisa A. Barnett
Production: Vicki Kasabian
Cover design: Jenny Jensen Greenleaf
Cover artwork: Todd Schaefer
Typesetter: Argosy
Manufacturing: Steve Bernier

Printed in the United States of America on acid-free paper
07 06 05 04 03   DA   1 2 3 4 5

ontents

And what of LSD? Is it just a drug or the reason a group of children wore flowers in their hair, had stars in the eyes, and thought they could change the world? If they knew then what they know now, would they still have tasted those sweetened drops or would they have lain down in the transcendental river of reality and let it wash them away—daisies and all?

What a crazy time that was. Whoo! But did we dig it then and do we dig it now? We do. And if I meet up with Scott Miller in St. Louis, I definitely will say thanks for letting me put the flowers back into my hair and keep the starlight in my eyes for two summers now. And I'll probably let him know that I dig all of the time he spent researching those cats and their message, so we could stay true to their power. Boom boom, beep beep.

And so maybe they really will change the world after all—just not as quickly as they had hoped because they didn't foresee the need to hand the daisy-powered baton to the next generation. And so maybe the journey of these past two summers of love are not at the beginning or the end but just another piece of that movement. And maybe when Scott and the rest of the tribe look in the mirror they'll notice the stars and they'll keep on passing out flowers.

Our destination is the same—our journey is where it's at and we all know where it's at. Let the sun shine in. Peace and love.

—Uchenna Ogu
Osage Tribe
St. Louis productions of *Hair,* 2000, 2001

Let the Sun Shine In

Mystic Crystal Revelations

It is an obscene and yet serene parade of shaggy-headed black and white people, coming, going, sometimes angry, sometimes sweet, sometimes bitterly truthful. Singing really good songs like "Aquarius" and "Let the Sun Shine In." People making love. Black people doing both their own thing and a white thing. White people doing their own thing, a black thing, and their forefather's thing. Sodomy. Love. Pot. Black-white sex/love. Black-black love/sex. Homosexual love/sex. The flag, endeared and chided. The war, ignobled and dishonored. A mockery of self. People nude and spiritual. Spirited people in raggedy, kooky clothes. A love-knock at the Supremes. An immortalization of James Brown. Shiny, glittery costumes. Psychedelic lighting. A love affair between the cast and the audience.

Ebony *magazine, May 1970*

The lyric to "Aquarius" talks of "harmony and understanding, sympathy and trust abounding, no more falsehood or derision, golden, living dreams of visions, mystic, crystal revelation, and the mind's true liberation." And it's not kidding. That stuff is real to anyone who's actually done *Hair*. And for those of us who've gone there, we wish the rest of the world could go there too. Especially now. There's a reason *Hair* was called "The American Tribal Love-Rock Musical."

In 1967, Gerome Ragni and James Rado wrote the refrain, "Let the sun shine, let the sun shine in, the sun shine in." It was the last stanza of a song they called "The Flesh Failures," with music by Galt MacDermot, and they meant every word. They were begging the world to turn back before it was too late. Those words became the stirring final anthem of their musical *Hair*, and that refrain gained worldwide popularity, both from the show and from The Fifth Dimension's recording of "Aquarius" and "Let the Sun Shine In," released in 1969.

Broadway tribe member Andre De Shields said in VH-1's Behind the Music documentary about *Hair*, "When you change your mind, you change your life. And that's what the hippie culture was all about." Michael Butler said, "I could see *Hair* every night and not be bored. It's like going to church for me. If it was the only accomplishment that I've done, I'd be perfectly happy. I don't know a theatre piece that has been as strong in this way for every one of us involved in it. I do feel it's a gift of God."

It's impossible to describe the experience of performing *Hair* to someone who hasn't done it. I was highly skeptical of the many people who told me their lives were changed by working on this show.

Until I directed productions in St. Louis in 2000 and 2001.

From the choosing of a tribe name to the overwhelming rush of emotion in the show's finale—every single night—performing the show is an experience unlike any other. Not only does it bond each member of the tribe to every other member (and this includes actors, director, designers, musicians, tech people), but it bonds each tribe to all the other tribes around the world, past, present, and future. It centers people, changes them, guides them toward balance in their lives, steers them back to paths in their lives they've forgotten or abandoned, helps them toward a deeper spirituality. Even the most cynical among us is transformed by *Hair*. It holds a mystical, primal power that is nearly impossible to explain. Just as it is utterly unique in so many concrete ways, it is just as unique in all the unexplainable ways.

Despite *Hair*'s apparent vulgarity and simplicity and sexual frankness, it really does work magic on people. And maybe the transcendence of *Hair* can be partially explained this way. Humans seem to have an endless hunger for knowing the unknowable, understanding that which cannot be understood. Our hopelessly insufficient human language can never *begin* to express all that is eternal and infinite and sublime about existence. That's what poetry is for, language that reaches beyond our normal capabilities, that expresses that which can't be literally expressed, that must be penetrated and explored and experienced from within. And that's what *Hair* does. The human hunger for transcendence is no less voracious today than it was in the 1960s. The experience of performing or watching *Hair* on stage works like the greatest human poetry, like Eliot or Shakespeare, by taking language beyond its literal meaning, coupling it with music, that most ineffable, most abstract of all languages, and exploring those mysteries we all yearn to understand. Why are we here? Is there a God? What is death? What lies beyond this world? What do we leave behind? *Hair* dares to go there. *Hair* dares to tell us that we don't need priests to explore those questions and we don't need the revealed word of human religion. We ourselves are divine and have every right to that exploration. And if we ask why we're here, then as actors, directors, and other theatre artists, we must ask why we make theatre. If we want to make theatre that counts, if we want to leave something of worth behind, if we want to connect to people in meaningful ways, how better than to present a work like *Hair*?

Because my theatre company closed our second production of the show just ten days before the terrorist attacks on the World Trade Center towers and the Pentagon in September 2001, the show shaped profoundly how we reacted to that event. We talked a lot about it among our tribe. We felt as if we all had an additional shield against the terror of the attack on America, a shield the rest of the country didn't know about—as Hallmarky as it may sound, we had the power and the peace of *Hair* to get us through. We had *Hair*'s belief in the good of people in general and the good of Americans in particular, in the strength of what's right, in its call to nonviolent action against evil, even in our own country and its faith in the search for higher truths, and maybe most of all, in the profundity of the bond among our tribe. But *Hair* also put us in a difficult spot, because it had genuinely convinced most of us that peace was *always* the answer, that war was *always* wrong. And though we felt the overwhelming rage most Americans felt in the weeks and months that followed the attacks, we also felt that more killing in response was not the answer. Because of *Hair* and the research we had done while we worked on the show, we saw parallels between Vietnam and the new War on Terror. We knew that nothing in this arena was ever black-and-white. We knew America is rarely blameless, that much of the world considers America a big imperialist bully, and that opposing war is not unpatriotic no matter what rabid flag wavers might tell us. America should have learned all those lessons in the 1960s, but apparently it had not. Still, what *was* the answer? Should the terrorists go unpunished? Should the attacks go unanswered? And yet, weren't the attacks themselves a response to past U.S. aggressions and our not-so-subtle brand of imperialism? If we killed in response to their killing in response to our killing, wouldn't they just attack us again? Where and when could the cycle of tragedy and violence ever end? We had no answers.

But the biggest difference I noticed between my fellow tribe members and everyone else was what we saw in the aftermath of September 11. As others suddenly realized that the world is infinitely crueler and colder than they thought, as others retreated into fear, our tribe realized how much kinder and more selfless the world is than we thought. As others realized how alone they are, our tribe realized how connected we all are. Where others saw the evil of the attack, we saw the incredible, overwhelming kindness everyone showed one another as the attack was underway and afterward. A handful of men perpetrated an act of terror, but millions of Americans displayed kindness and patriotism and solidarity. The act of terror took months, maybe years of planning, but the kindness took no planning at all. Even the people in the Trade Center buildings, as they made their way down the staircases after the initial impact, showed incredible calm and kindness toward one another. Hundreds of New Yorkers made their way toward Ground Zero immediately to volunteer their help. Thousands of emergency workers from across our country went to New York immediately to help in the rescue effort. Millions of Americans sent donations to the September 11 charities. Most of the nations of the world sent their condolences and warm wishes to America. Where others saw humankind at its worst, our tribe saw humankind at its very best.

The other thing that gave me any comfort was the hope that maybe this was the catalyst we needed for a new revolution. Michael Butler, the original Broadway producer of *Hair*, told me when he flew in to see our production that he believes the social upheaval of the 1960s is coming back and he wants the hundreds of thousands of *Hair* tribe members worldwide to be a driving force in this new movement. He has collected tens of thousands of names and addresses (physical and e-mail) and wants to bring the *Hair* tribes together into a positive, social force that will pick up where the hippies left off, to finally make real, meaningful change in our society. Certainly, when the United States declared war on September 11, every one of us in the Osage Tribe saw parallels to Vietnam and we wondered how Michael knew.

Hair returns us to our primitive tribal roots. The circle plays such an important role in the staging patterns of most productions of *Hair*, both consciously and unconsciously; it takes us back to the time before recorded history when humans would gather around the fire and tell stories, the true roots of theatre. Now, once again, in our increasingly mechanized, depersonalized world, the *Hair* tribes come together to sit, stand, and dance in a circle, to tell stories, to reach back to the beginning and find the essence of what makes us human and what makes us still so very tribal. In some productions, the audience is even seated in a circle around the stage, bringing them into that experience as well. *Hair* is wildly experimental (even by today's standards) and extremely sophisticated, but also extraordinarily simple and pure at its core, and it's that simplicity and purity, that innocence even in the midst of the four-letter words and nudity, that makes it so universal, so powerful, so utterly unforgettable.

Is *Hair* dated? It's true that nudity and four-letter words on stage are hardly shocking today. But that's only an issue if you believe that *Hair*'s primary aim is to shock, which is not the case. Certainly, *Hair* does not have the same impact on an audience today that it did when it was originally produced. But neither does *Show Boat* or *West Side Story* or *Carousel* or *Rent*. No, *Hair* does not have the *same* impact; it has a *new* impact. The nudity and cursing no longer shock. Today, it's the political passion that shocks, the idea of civil disobedience, the idea that young people care about their world and their government. That was a given when *Hair* debuted in 1967, but having survived the self-involved 1980s and 1990s, when the idea of a youth movement seemed distinctly quaint and old-fashioned, today *Hair* describes the *new* youth movement that rejects racism more strongly than ever, that rejects sexual oppression more than ever, that demands a government be held accountable. What shocks us today is the idea of theatre whose goal is to make an audience *think* and *feel*, whose goal is to change minds and hearts, to move an audience to action. The distractions of the shock of nudity and profanity are now thankfully put aside, allowing audiences to focus more fully on the things in *Hair* that really matter.

In September 2002, Peter Jennings and ABC produced a documentary miniseries called *In Search of America*, and one episode followed a production of *Hair* at Fairview High School, in Boulder, Colorado, done the previous September. New York's *Daily News* opined, "But by far, the installment not to miss—the one that should have opened *In Search of America*—is Thursday's, which tracks a high school production of the musical *Hair*, with unexpectedly emotional and meaningful results. At first, it looks like a typical visit to a typical, if privileged and somewhat segregated, high school in Boulder, Colorado. Teenagers, most of them white, seem to be coasting without many concerns, and they seem not to relate to the school's musical. In fact, teachers have to import some parents to lecture about the 1960s, when *Hair* made its Broadway debut. Students are nervous about kissing and touching, even in an edited and nudity-free staging, and just don't get some of the issues involved: the passion for embracing and understanding different races and cultures, the fear and loathing of the draft, and the dissatisfaction that made some people drop out or protest. *In Search of America* followed the rehearsals for months—and somewhere in there came September 11, which changed everything. By the time these students and teachers at Fairview High School mounted their show, not only had the play grown on them, it changed them—and many of their parents. And this story is likely to touch you as well." Is *Hair* dated? No.

Perhaps *The Journal of Popular Culture* summed it all up best. Irving Buchen wrote, in 1969, "I have sought to take *Hair* seriously (some may claim too much so) because I take the prospect of revolution seriously, especially one that expresses itself exclusively as feeling and action. And what convinces me that *Hair* points to a radical future is that it has a strong, urgent, and often accurate sense of what is evil." After September 11, 2001, that is perhaps more important than ever.

In the Beginning . . .

On February 2, 1962, the moon, Mercury, Venus, Mars, Jupiter, and Saturn all aligned in the constellation Aquarius. All seven of these heavenly bodies had not come together for 2,500 years. Many people believed it was the dawning of a new age, the age of Aquarius, symbolizing a pooling of everyone's creativity, an age of communalism.

The 1960s were certainly a time for experimentation in both musical and nonmusical theatre. There were mainstream experiments in musical theatre like *Cabaret* and *Man of La Mancha*, and decidedly nonmainstream experiments like *Anyone Can Whistle, Marat/Sade, Jacques Brel, Oh What a Lovely War, Celebration, Promenade*, and of course the rock musical *Hair*.

When *Hair* opened, Michael Smith of *The Village Voice* called it "downtown, dirty, ballsy, and outrageous." *Time* magazine wrote, "This musical is a cross between a Dionysian revel and an old-fashioned revival meeting. The religion that *Hair* preaches, and often screeches, is flower power, pot, and protest." *Saturday Review* said, "Director Tom O'Horgan is pushing the medium to new limits by moving away from the verbality of multisensual theater. Instead of finding conventional musical-comedy performers to impersonate hippies, he has encouraged a bunch of mainly hippie performers inventively to explore their own natures with song and dance." In *The Journal of Popular Culture*, Buchen wrote, "*Hair* cannot be cut short as mere sensationalism; nudity there is, but it is selective, functional, and even discrete. It is not the new drama of assault or insult, although the audience is never immune from incursions into its midst. It is radical but not violent; eclectic but not chaotic; sexually free wheeling but not perverse." He called it "an authentic glimpse into a preverbal state—perhaps, into the origins of drama itself as chant and dance."

John J. O'Connor wrote in *The Wall Street Journal*, "No matter the reaction to the content . . . I suspect the form will be important to the history of the American musical." And it was, paving the way for the nonlinear concept musicals that dominated musical theatre innovation in the 1970s: *Company, Follies, A Chorus Line, Working*, and others. And yet, some Broadway establishment figures refused then and now to accept this radical departure. Even today, some people can't see past the appearance of chaos and randomness to the brilliant construction and sophisticated imagery underneath. In 1996, while reviewing *Hair's* godchild, the rock musical *Rent*, Howard Kissel wrote in the New York *Daily News* that *Hair* had been nothing more than "formless amateurism." Even as recently as the summer of 2000, one hapless reviewer in St. Louis wrote of the show, "*Hair* remains a musical theatre anomaly, a freaked-out mishmash of psychedelic-babble. . . . You'd have to be stoned to have written it and it would help if you're watching it."

In the 1960s, the artists of off Broadway and off off Broadway were complaining that the professional (i.e., Broadway) theatre was dead, and even worse, that it was boring. They saw that the tightly ordered, regimented, safe, compartmentalized commercial theatre had no worthwhile relation to the chaotic, tumultuous real world of the 1960s. Socially conscious, political theatre had been born in the 1930s with the Group Theatre, but that company had only lasted ten years, and though its influence was still felt, American theatre had fallen back into complacency. But the tumult of the real world in the 1960s was bleeding into the world of the theatre. A true theatrical revolution was afoot. Arthur Sainer, an off off Broadway experimental playwright, wrote, "The changes occurred because the theatre as we had known it, the theatre of character, of problems and resolutions, the theatre of beings uttering intelligently formed, balanced sentences, the theatre of significant scenes, of fortuitous events, was no longer working for many of us. . . . We began to understand in the 60s that the words in plays, that the physical beings in plays, that the events in plays, were too often evasions, too often artifices that have to do not with the truths but with semblances."

Hair was the revolution—the commercially successful revolution—they had been waiting for, that took all their off off Broadway experiments, which only a select few ever saw, and set those experiments down right in the middle of the Great White Way not only to critical acclaim but also commercial and popular success. With very little plot, a unit set, plenty of four-letter words, explicit sexual content, ritual, drugs, lyrics that didn't rhyme, music that didn't follow the rules, and the sound of genuine rock, this musical knocked Broadway on its collective ass. Not only did many of the lyrics not rhyme, but many of the songs didn't really have endings, just a slowing down and stopping, so the audience didn't know when to applaud. Other songs segued directly into the next number so the audience didn't have time to applaud. The show rejected every convention of Broadway, of traditional theatre in general, and of the American musical in particular. And it was unerringly brilliant.

Most surprising of all, it was an enormous hit. Director Tom O'Horgan said at the time that he saw *Hair* as a once-in-a-lifetime opportunity to create "a theatre form whose demeanor, language, clothing, dance, and even its name accurately reflect a social epoch in full explosion." *Hair* acted as a launching pad for the careers of Diane Keaton, Melba Moore, Donna Summer, Tim Curry, Nell Carter, Peter Gallagher, Joe Montegna, Ben Vereen, Cliff DeYoung, Meat Loaf, Richard O'Brien, and many other performers who went on to great success.

Hair criticizes and satirizes racism, discrimination, war, violence, pollution, sexual repression, and other societal evils. It is a psychedelic (in the true sense of the word) musical, reproducing in a way the mind-bending, often disorienting sensation of an LSD or peyote trip, perhaps the only such musical ever on Broadway. The show is made up of a barrage of images, often very surrealistic, often overwhelming, coming at the audience fast and furiously, not always following logically; but when taken together, those images form a wonderful, unified, and ultimately comprehensible whole. At its best, the show really can cause the kind of euphoria in its audience that one usually associates with psychedelic drugs. As with most satire, *Hair* makes fun of racism, war, sex, and other things by carrying them to ridiculous extremes (as in the songs "Sodomy" and "Colored Spade"). *Hair* shocks the audience (though that is not really its goal) by challenging what they believe, by showing how absurd, how offensive, how nonsensical, and in some cases, how dangerous are the behavior and language that society calls "normal." Tommy Smothers, half of the famous 1960s duo the Smothers Brothers and one of *Hair*'s producers in Los Angeles, said in one interview, "The shock of the show was its totality, its statement. It was peace and love and rock and roll." No Broadway show had ever done that before.

And the show asks some good questions: Why did we send American soldiers halfway around the world to Vietnam to kill strangers when there was no direct threat to our country? Why can't we talk openly about sex? Why are certain words "dirty" and other words that mean the same thing acceptable? Why are there so many offensive words for black people but hardly any for white people? Why are so many straight people interested in what gay people do in private? If the Constitution guarantees free speech, why can't we burn the flag? Is it right to protest and refuse to follow laws that are unjust?

It also asks more subtle questions: Does a theatre piece have to tell a linear story? Does a musical have to tell a love story? Must an audience be separate and passive? Must a show be comforting and safe? Can a musical address serious issues as effectively as theatre that lacks music? Do costumes have to be pretty? Do lyrics have to rhyme? Can you say "fuck" in a Broadway musical?

Hair was never pretentious enough to presume to answer the social questions, but it answered resoundingly many of the questions about the nature of theatrical art. At any rate, just asking the questions was enough.

2 Here Are Your Seeds, Baby

Hair was so much a part of its time, such an inextricable piece of the zeitgeist of the sixties, that appreciation of the show today hovers precariously on a precipice of amused indulgence. *Weren't those hippies something!* we think. *Boy, that must've been fun to live back then!* We forget that sons and brothers and boyfriends were going half a world away to die. We forget that African Americans were still refused service at establishments across the country. We forget that the hippies (the serious ones, anyway) honestly believed they could change the world. And who's to say they didn't?

We forget that the hippies loved America in their own way every bit as much as their parents, maybe more. The hippies believed in an idea President John F. Kennedy was planning to articulate in the speech he never got to deliver on November 22, 1963. In that speech, he wrote, "We are in this country watchmen on the walls of freedom. We ask, therefore, that we may be worthy of our power and responsibility, that we may achieve the ancient vision of peace on earth, goodwill toward men." The peace movement was not an aberration. It was where America was headed. Instead of turning a blind eye to America's faults and indulgences and sins, the younger generation wanted to fix what was wrong, to return America to the shining possibility its founding fathers saw so clearly. They wanted

America to be the best it could be. And certainly, America was *not* the best it could be in the 1960s.

We forget that severe prejudice flourished in America in the sixties, racial and sexual prejudice and so much more. Lynchings continued in the South. Black farmers often worked land owned by rich white landlords to whom they were perpetually indebted, and they were essentially still trapped in (a slightly different form of) slavery. Women and gays were very much second-class citizens, both socially and legally. In 1953 alone, more than nine hundred State Department employees were fired for the perversion of being (or appearing to be) gay. The "Red menace" of Communism was often tied tightly to the "homosexual menace." Gay meant Red, which meant traitor. The folks with "America—Love It or Leave It" on their bumpers were all straight white males.

We forget that the philosophy of drug use was not new. For centuries, the most advanced and the most revered civilizations used hallucinogenic drugs in their rituals and religious ceremonies. Marijuana had been mainstream in America for decades. And the serious hippies rejected drugs that shut the mind down, like alcohol. To them, drugs were a path to expanded consciousness, to the answers to our problems, and to God.

Any understanding of the sixties in America—and of *Hair*— must be built upon an understanding of all the influences that lay underneath: the hippie culture and philosophy, drugs, politics, the war in Vietnam, the sexual revolution, the experimental theatre movement, the Beat poets, and so much else. What follows is a sampling of the seeds of the revolution that was *Hair*.

The Hippies

The hippies of the sixties were the second-generation successors to the "Beat" movement of the fifties. (Interestingly, later on many hippies didn't call themselves "hippies"—they called themselves "freaks.") They comprised a counterculture movement that included many separate submovements—the drug culture, nudists and naturalists, vegetarians, "Jesus freaks," communes, environmentalists, Krishna followers, mystics, and many others. The thing that united them was their rejection of the mainstream culture, the culture of their parents, the culture of racially segregated, prefabricated suburbia. In 1967, Ralph Gleason wrote in *Evergreen Review* that the hippies "are not just dropping out into Limbo or Nirvana. They are building a new set of values, a new structure, a new society. . . . [They] are attacking the very principle upon which this society is built: It is more sacred to make money than to be a good man."

The hippie movement started in the early sixties, and by 1969 many hippies were in their thirties and older. In fact, the older hippies were sometimes revered as tribal wise men. The hippies were about nonviolence, about individualism, about a rejection of materialism, about spirituality but also a rejection of institutionalized religion, and above all about the desire to reach a higher, purer level of consciousness. Their drug use was not just an escape; it was also a means to help them find the spirituality they believed their parents had lost in the meaningless hypocrisy of organized religion. (In 1967, Father James Kavanaugh published his book *A Modern Priest Looks at His Outdated Church.*) Looking at their parents and the rest of the "older generation," hippies saw evidence that mainstream religions had reduced religious experience, the act of living through faith, to nothing more than symbols and metaphors, subverting and short-circuiting the religious experience itself. They believed that mainstream religious traditions and rituals got in the way of true faith and the search for ultimate truths. And because more young Americans than ever before were attending college and while there studying other world religions, they were finding that the creation/Genesis story, the sacrifice/crucifixion and resurrection of Jesus Christ, the miracles performed by Jesus, and most of the other central stories of Christianity had shown up in other world religions long before. Though this did not automatically discount all of Christianity for them, it did throw its claims of absolute and unique truth into question. As a result, many young adults began exploring the older Eastern religions. John Lennon said in an interview with London's *Evening Standard*, "Christianity will go. It will vanish and shrink. I needn't argue about that; I'm right and will be proved right. We're more popular than Jesus right now. I don't know which will go first, rock 'n' roll or Christianity. Jesus was all right, but his disciples were thick and ordinary. It's them twisting it that ruins it for me." In response, across the American South, public burnings of Beatles albums were organized by fundamentalist preachers and radio stations.

Most hippies differentiated between "good" and "bad" drugs. The "good" drugs were mind-expanding, psychedelic drugs like marijuana, peyote, and LSD that helped them find peace and spirituality ("the mind's true liberation"). The "bad" drugs were those used only for escape, like alcohol, nicotine, tranquilizers (like Valium), cocaine, and heroin. In 1969, Gallup conducted a survey of students on fifty-seven American college campuses. Thirty-one percent (between ten and twelve million students) had smoked pot, and 10 to 15 percent (one or two million) had used LSD. Those numbers have changed only slightly since. In 1997, 49 percent had smoked pot and 14 percent had used LSD. And, as in the sixties, far fewer had used "bad" drugs, with only 8 percent having tried cocaine and only 2 percent having tried heroin. These numbers raise two interesting questions. First, why do the mind-expanding drugs continue to be so popular and the mind-numbing drugs so much less popular? And also, if that many college kids were using mind-expanding drugs in 1969 and America has not collapsed, and if so few kids today are using the "bad" drugs, is the drug crisis as real and as pervasive as many would have us believe?

The abuse of prescription drugs by the "antidrug" adults is satirized in Act I of *Hair* as two mothers (played by men) bemoan their rebellious daughters and Berger responds by offering tranquilizers to several famous authority figures who were then having trouble with rebellious kids—Rabbi Schultz (a high-profile Jewish political figure), the Rockefeller Foundation, President Nixon, Vice-President Humphrey, and the Pope. The hippies condemned this kind of drug use. They believed that by making alcohol and tranquilizers their drugs of choice, the older generation had betrayed their progeny, choosing to hide, to ignore, rather than to engage with the problems of the world. The drug-trip song "Walking in Space" in Act II of *Hair* says explicitly that the reasons for taking the drugs are self-awareness, finding truth, and finding God. Just look at the lyric:

> *My soul is in orbit*
> *With God, face to face.*
> . . .
> *On a rocket to the fourth dimension,*
> *Total self-awareness the intention.*

We have to ask why we have such restrictive and such arbitrary rules about drugs. Is it because once we taste the liberation of mind-expanding substances, once we discover the Great Truths, we'll be harder to control? Why do the adults who drink like fishes at cocktail parties so self-righteously condemn marijuana? Why do they so strongly condemn all drugs, when so many other cultures highly value the ritual use of hallucinogenic drugs to achieve a higher level of consciousness and to find God? Paul McCartney said in one sixties interview, "God is the space between us. God is the table in front of you. It just happened I realized all this through weed." The song "Initials" in *Hair* makes one of the strongest and most interesting— though perhaps most overlooked—statements in the show. Through a series of initials, it draws a direct line from President Johnson (LBJ) to LSD, laughing at the establishment's paranoiac fear of drugs and suggesting that if the establishment would open its collective mind to the use of hallucinogenic drugs it too might find the answers to all the seemingly insurmountable problems it has created. The song's lyric suggests that if Johnson would just go into the streets and talk to America's youth, he would find out that they hold the answers. And the song ends with comic references to the FBI and the CIA, who, in the hysterical anti-Commie cold war atmosphere of sixties America, were conducting experiments with mind-altering drugs as possible chemical warfare agents.

Change, Change, Change

The youth movement was about to take off in the late fifties, and as if heralding this new age, John F. Kennedy, the youngest president in U.S. history, was elected in the fall of 1959. The "baby boomer" children growing up in the fifties had all the consumer goods they could want but found little to feed their souls. They had had extremely permissive childhoods and were then expected to fit into a repressively conformist adult world. Their parents taught them conservative values while at the same time engaging in social drinking at levels not seen since the 1920s. Also, many more kids than ever before were being sent to college, where they were learning to question everything, to form their own opinions about the world. They found that the liberal arts education that their parents so wanted for them turned them into highly educated men and women with no real-world skills, lots of unanswered existential questions, and no preparation to get a job and start a family. Even worse, these kids left college with endless possibilities before them—too many possibilities, it turned out.

Whereas earlier generations had been locked into taking over family businesses, the baby boomers had more freedom in choosing their futures but no guideposts; in many cases, the wide array of choices proved overwhelming.

Along with all this, the black civil rights movement was gaining steam, and all these disillusioned kids found a strong, viable model for social protest. Following the example of Martin Luther King Jr. and other great black leaders, the youth of America, especially those on college campuses, started protesting all the things they saw wrong with America: racism, environmental destruction, poverty, sexism and sexual repression, violence at home and the war in Vietnam, depersonalization from new technologies, and corruption in politics. The hippies' predecessors, the Beat generation, had been a far less political counterculture. But the escalation of the war in Vietnam, the expansion of the draft, more aggressively enforced drug laws, and increased antiloitering sweeps in parks and public spaces forced the hippies to become political, and a new underground press sprang up. Contrary to popular opinion, the hippies had great respect for America and believed that *they* were the true patriots, the only ones who genuinely wanted to save our country and make it the best it could be once again. In 1966, *Time* magazine's Man of the Year was the "Twenty-Five and Under Generation," the newest political force in America.

Another difference between the Beats and the hippies was the audience for their respective art. The Beats' chosen art forms were poetry and jazz, and they readily admitted that their art was elitist. The hippies, on the other hand, were determined to create art of the people, and their chosen art form, rock/folk music, was by its definition populist. Due in large part to Bob Dylan, country music also became a big part of the hippie music movement (as represented in *Hair* by "Don't Put It Down"). But possibly the biggest difference between the music of the hippies and the music of the Beats was that the hippies' music was often very angry, its anger directed at those who would prostitute the Constitution, who would sell America out, who would betray what America stood for—in other words, their parents and the government.

In 1967, twenty thousand people gathered in Golden Gate Park, in San Francisco, for the world's first "be-in." (The term *be-in* became very popular and was later parodied in the title of the TV show "Laugh-In.") As be-ins continued around the country, they attracted not only hippies but also gawkers who had heard about the be-ins and wanted to see what they were all about. In *Hair*, Jeanie refers to these gawkers when she asks "What's going on inside all those little *Daily News* heads?" New York's *Daily News* was then and still is a sensationalist tabloid newspaper that panders to its readers' taste for the most lurid, most shocking stories. Jeanie and the tribe are making fun of the people who read the *Daily News*, who came to the be-ins to be shocked and titillated, looking for orgies, nudity, rampant drug use, and mass arrests, which they rarely found.

Despite the hippies' anticapitalist leanings and playing along with their populist intentions, major record labels quickly got the (unintended) message of the be-ins and immediately signed several San Francisco bands to gigantic advances. After all, American teenagers were a whole new consumer market, spending annually twelve million of their own money and thirteen million of their parents' money, buying more than half of all movie tickets sold in America and nearly half of all audio recordings, as well as more than half of all soft drinks and twenty percent of all cosmetics. Twenty percent of all American high school students owned their own cars. The record labels and other businesses wanted in on this cash cow.

In early 1967, Brian Jones of the Rolling Stones told one interviewer that things were changing, that the world "was about to enter the age of Aquarius. There is a young revolution in thought and manner about to take place." By 1967, college courses were undergoing a sea change. Dartmouth offered a course called "An Investigation into Sex." The University of Pennsylvania offered "Analogues to the LSD Experience." DePauw offered "Guerilla Warfare." Brooklyn College offered "The Origins and Meanings of Black Power." And Stanford offered a course called "American Youth in Revolt." Colleges across America were also offering courses in Asian religions and theology. High school teachers were teaching Bob Dylan's lyrics as poetry in English classes, and psychedelic artists like Peter Max were designing mainstream advertisements.

Jim Rado and Gerry Ragni gave *Hair* its title because long hair was the hippies' flag—their "freak flag," some of them called it—their symbol not only of rebellion but also of new possibilities, of the rejection of discrimination and restrictive gender roles (a philosophy celebrated in the song "My Conviction"). It symbolized equality between men and women. In addition to their long hair, the hippies' chosen clothing also made statements. Drab work clothes (jeans, work shirts, pea coats) were a rejection of materialism. Clothing from other cultures, particularly third world and native American, represented their awareness of the global community and their rejection of U.S. imperialism and selfishness. Simple cotton dresses and other natural fabrics were a rejection of synthetics, a return to natural things and simpler times. Some hippies wore old World War II or Civil War jackets as way of co-opting the symbols of war into their newfound philosophy of nonviolence. Much to the dismay of hardcore "patriots" of the time, the hippies also loved incorporating the U.S. flag into their clothing—making shirts or jackets out of the flag, using the flag to patch their jeans—both to show their love of America and to publicly reject the very strict, very arbitrary rules for how that love can be expressed. Tie-dyed clothing, which people today connect inextricably to the hippie culture, wasn't as widespread as we think. Tie-dye was mostly a west coast phenomenon and didn't make it to the east coast (where *Hair* is set) until the seventies.

Nudity was also a big part of the hippie culture, both as a rejection of the sexual repression of their parents and also as a statement about naturalism, spirituality, honesty, openness, and freedom. Jim Rado says *Hair's* nude scene was inspired by an event he and Ragni witnessed in Central Park. The naked body was seen by the hippies as beautiful, something to be celebrated and appreciated, not scorned and hidden. They saw their bodies and their sexuality as gifts, not as "dirty" things. But black poet Don Lee said, "*Hair* is indicative of the whole white theater scene. The white man's own limitations are heightened by the fact that nudity is the only attractive thing he has going. The nudity aspect of white theater is an important comment on the state of the Union, and *Hair* is one of the prime vehicles to make that comment."

In 1969, after *Hair* had been running for a while, Clive Barnes of the *New York Times* returned to the show and wrote a follow-up review in which he said, "People say the show is dirty. Rubbish. It is as clean as Tide and not half so chemical. Members of the cast do occasionally use naughty words, but in a quite childlike fashion. They do—for one moment of social and esthetic revolt—take off their clothes if they wish to. But this is not obscene. It is also totally asexual. If you are proposing to go to *Hair* for sexual stimulation you don't need a theater ticket, you need treatment."

What most people don't realize is that the counterculture of the 1960s is still with us. In 1994, when the new Speaker of the House,

Newt Gingrich, celebrated the Republicans' takeover of the U.S. Congress, he said, "There are profound things that went wrong starting with [Lyndon Johnson's] Great Society [programs] and the counterculture, and until we address them head-on we're going to have problems." Gingrich and his followers despise and fear nearly everything the sixties gave us, feminism, gay rights, sexual freedom, reproductive rights, affirmative action, environmentalism, recreational drugs, and many of America's social programs. Conservatives want stability, a return to the "traditional values" of the fifties, a time of calm and social stability that never really existed. The time they look back on with such fondness was a time of unending oppression of women, African Americans (and all other minorities), gay Americans, and the poor. It was a time of profound hypocrisy, both sexual and moral, and boiling unrest lay ready to blow the top off of suburban America.

To conservatives, the counterculture of the sixties represents a frighteningly continuous shifting of social roles and values, a shifting that the conservatives keep trying to halt with no success, a shifting that continues today. These conservatives demonize America's rich religious and spiritual diversity—a diversity our founding fathers saw as invaluable—and call it "moral relativism." They continue to claim that America was founded on "Christian principles" even though the majority of Americans have stopped attending church, have abandoned organized religion, and even though most of the founding fathers were Deists, not Christians. The conservatives continue to demonize the use of drugs in America, ignoring the simple truth that mind-expanding drugs like LSD and pot continue to be far more popular than the drugs that shut the mind down, like cocaine or heroin, refusing to ask the obvious questions: what value do people find in mind-expanding drugs and are they *really* harmful? Perhaps they fear LSD, mescaline, and peyote because these drugs reveal the lies of capitalist "Christian" America, the lie that money, position, and power matter.

A Really, Really Brief Look at the War

In its first, 1967 version, *Hair* was primarily about the war in Vietnam, the longest war in American history. It was during the rewrites made when the show moved to Broadway in 1968 that other issues were added and made more prominent. Nevertheless, Vietnam was a major issue in the hippie movement, and though its prominence was reduced in the second version of the show, it still formed the backdrop of its only real story line, that of Claude going off to war. An understanding of the background of the war is therefore important to an understanding of *Hair*. It's also important to remember that people still disagree not only on interpretations of and motivations for the war but also on facts about the war. It's impossible to find two references today that tell precisely the same story.

Vietnam had been a possession of France since the late nineteenth century. During World War II, the French gave Vietnam to the Japanese. Toward the end of the war, a Vietnamese leader named Ho Chi Minh established a government headquartered in Hanoi, in the northern part of the country, with a constitution based loosely on the U.S. Constitution (he was an ardent admirer of Thomas Jefferson), though with Communist leanings. But after the war was over, Churchill insisted that Vietnam should return to French "ownership," against the wishes of the Vietnamese people, and the French invaded the country to take it back.

In the early 1950s, a Vietnamese Communist faction under the leadership of Ho Chi Minh rose up against the French and finally drove them back out of Vietnam. The United States first got involved in 1950 by helping to fund the French war against the Vietnamese. An international conference in Geneva, Switzerland, in 1954 negotiated a cease-fire and split the country in two, leaving the north half of the country to Ho Chi Minh. The conference also demanded that free elections be held in 1956 to reunify the country. But the leaders in the south refused to hold the elections because they knew how widespread support was for the increasingly Communist Ho Chi Minh. Some U.S. politicians were so terrified by Communism, so obsessed with its perceived threat, that they believed the United States had to support this refusal. These politicians believed there was a secret international alliance of Communist countries, and that if Vietnam fell to the Communists, they would then systematically take over the world, country by country, until the United States itself fell to Communism. Of course, these politicians were wrong—there was no such international threat or alliance.

Based on this unfounded fear, the United States went in and set up a pseudodemocratic puppet government in South Vietnam in 1956, claiming rule over the entire country; but the North

Vietnamese refused to recognize this government (it actually had very little power outside the city of Saigon). To add to the tension, some of the South Vietnamese saw the Americans as no different than the French, just another foreign power who wanted to control them. In the early sixties, a coalition of South Vietnamese Communist groups, called the Vietcong (which were basically independent of the Communists in North Vietnam, though connected in some ways) rose up against the U.S. puppet government as well.

After John F. Kennedy's assassination in 1963, Lyndon Johnson inherited a U.S. commitment to South Vietnam, despite his strong previously voiced doubts that South Vietnam could ever win a war against the North and that the U.S. public would ever accept direct American involvement. A few secret bombing raids were conducted by the U.S. in North Vietnam, but soon direct involvement was the only choice if America was to stay involved.

In 1964, the North Vietnamese (apparently) fired on U.S. personnel, and President Johnson convinced Congress to give him free rein to take "all necessary measures" to retaliate, an act that was unprecedented and arguably un-Constitutional. Some historians believe Johnson needed the war in order to jump-start dormant patriotism and to galvanize the American people behind his social programs and his dream of the Great Society. Unfortunately, it didn't work the way he planned.

Johnson began by ordering the bombing of North Vietnam. Then in 1965, the United States sent the first combat ground troops—thirty-five hundred men—into South Vietnam to fight the two enemies, the Vietcong and the North Vietnamese. The U.S. also began strategic bombing raids over North Vietnam. Johnson sent government-sponsored speakers to dozens of American college campuses to try to diffuse early antiwar sentiment. But antiwar protests, marches, and demonstrations began in America around 1967, in large part because this was the first war ever broadcast on television, and that coverage wasn't what we're used to today, with correspondents reporting from the rooftops of hotels. During the Vietnam War, the reporters and cameramen went into combat along with the ground troops and beamed home pictures of blood and carnage, bringing the full horror of war into American living rooms. Most Americans had never seen war like this. It was real, and the televised footage put them right in the middle of it. The protests escalated and continued throughout the rest of the war. (The Pentagon learned its lesson and never allowed such open access to the press again—and, no surprise, there have been virtually no major antimilitary protests since.) Interestingly, many of the troops in Vietnam agreed with the antiwar protesters and began wearing antiwar symbols on their uniforms. Antiwar protests by U.S. troops in Vietnam escalated to the point of massive desertions and sometimes the murder of high-ranking officers. In 1967, the high-profile Vietnam Veterans Against the War was formed.

In 1967, a huge march on the Pentagon was organized, with protesters completely surrounding the Pentagon, holding hands and trying through mutual concentration to levitate the Pentagon (no kidding) as a show of power. They didn't succeed in their levitation attempt but the event shook the Johnson administration, changed policy, and led in certain ways to the disintegration of Johnson's presidency.

By 1969, with no victory in sight, President Nixon talked about plans for U.S. troop withdrawal, promising to end the war within three years. In 1973, a cease-fire was agreed to and most of the U.S. ground troops left Vietnam, but the bombing of North Vietnam continued. Eventually, in 1975, the North Vietnamese took Saigon, the biggest city in South Vietnam (renaming it Ho Chi Minh City), and effectively "won" the war, forcing the United States to pull out completely. Once the Communists took over, the U.S. politicians were proved wrong. Instead of Communism spreading across Asia and Europe, the Communist countries started fighting one another.

During the Vietnam War, more than 47,000 Americans were killed in action and more than 300,000 wounded in action. The South Vietnamese suffered about 200,000 killed and 500,000 wounded. The North Vietnamese and the Vietcong suffered about 900,000 killed and an unknown number wounded. More than a million Vietnamese civilians were killed. The financial cost of the war ended up at about two hundred billion dollars.

The legacy of the war is that America lost its innocence. It was no longer the unquestioned good guy in world affairs. The reception for troops returning from the war was not always friendly. Many Americans felt the war was immoral, and America's long-held image of itself as global champion of the oppressed was replaced by an image of America as bully, interfering where it had no business, killing innocent men, women, and children, and lying about it all to the public. Our eyes were opened.

Black and White

When the black tribe members in *Hair* sing "Dead End," we see too clearly the two Americas that existed in the sixties (and still exist today), the hurdles placed in front of African Americans, the double standard that prevented many black Americans from ever realizing the mythical American Dream that white politicians constantly invoked. Even in the music industry, where blacks seemed to have an easier time of it, African Americans often couldn't stay in the hotels in which they performed. Sam Phillips, owner of Sun Records, said in the late fifties, "If I could find a white man who had the Negro sound and the Negro feel, I could make a billion dollars." The sound was commercial but black faces were not.

The abolition of slavery had put some African Americans in even worse straits. Now they were out on their own, but they were facing profound bigotry and discrimination. Now they were responsible for their own financial survival and yet were treated just as badly as when they were slaves. The abolition of slavery conferred American citizenship on them only technically; they still had to contend with poll taxes, literacy requirements, segregation, selective prosecutions, lynchings, and other horrors. Bob Dylan's album *Highway 61 Revisited* was named for the highway many southern blacks took from the Mississippi Delta up to Chicago in hopes of finding new lives.

Racial activism began in earnest in the fifties and increased steadily throughout the sixties. Black American men had fought in World War II in unprecedented numbers, with some all-black regiments seeing more frontline fighting than any others. Upon their return, they foolishly expected their sacrifice for the country, their bravery in the name of America and democracy, would earn them real freedom, genuine first-class citizenship at last. They were wrong. Lynchings continued. Horrific oppression went on unabated. But their service in World War II had taught black men something important—how to stand up and fight for what's right. They came back energized and ready for the greatest and longest-overdue fight in American history, the fight for civil rights for African Americans. Political and social activists protested not only racial bigotry in America's laws and institutions but also in American hearts. African Americans and sympathetic white Americans staged sit-ins at segregated lunch counters, boycotted segregated buses, protested segregated colleges, and organized massive marches on southern towns over voting rights. These actions were often opposed, sometimes brutally, sometimes fatally.

In 1960, four blacks sat down at a "whites only" lunch counter and began a national trend, followed in that year alone by 70,000 black and white Americans staging sit-ins in more than a hundred cities. More than 250,000 people assembled in Washington, D.C., in 1963 to hear Martin Luther King Jr. deliver his now famous "I Have a Dream" speech. And yet, that same year the police of Birmingham, Mississippi, greeted King and his followers with fire hoses, police dogs, and cattle prods. In 1963 alone, 14,000 Americans were arrested in seventy-five southern cities during civil rights demonstrations. In 1964, 464,000 black students boycotted the New York City public schools, effectively ending segregation. Many people in the sixties believed that the escalating war on drugs was based more on racial fear than anything else, on the fear that African Americans would rise up and refuse to be controlled anymore. Since millions of well-to-do suburban white kids were smoking pot and were rarely arrested on drug charges, since the use of (mind-numbing) drugs was often more prevalent in ghettos and lower-income neighborhoods in response to economic oppression, many people believed that the war on drugs was merely a convenient disguise for a war on black America.

One restaurant owner in Atlanta, Lester Maddox, closed his restaurant in 1964 rather than be forced to serve blacks. Before he decided to close, he handed out pickaxe handles to customers to beat any blacks entering his establishment. Yet the protestors marched on. In 1962, Robert Kennedy appeared on national television and asked, "Are we to say to the world that this is the land of the free except for the Negroes?" That same year, the Students Nonviolent Coordinating Committee (SNCC) organized the Freedom Ballot and traveled throughout Alabama, Georgia, and Mississippi registering black voters.

Despite President Lyndon Johnson's support of the war in Vietnam, he was definitely a friend of the civil rights movement, and he fought for the Civil Rights Bill of 1964 and the Voting Rights Act of 1965. Yet it wasn't until 1967 that the U.S. Supreme Court finally struck down state laws against interracial marriage.

In 1966, the "Black Power" movement was born, taking its name from the hippies' "Flower Power" movement. The Black Power followers disagreed with Martin Luther King's pacifist agenda and wanted to pursue civil rights more aggressively. In fact, there was no consensus on how to achieve equality for African Americans. Some groups believed in peacefully working through the established system, including the NAACP, the Congress for Racial Equality (CORE), the Students Nonviolent Coordinating Committee (SNCC), and Martin Luther King's Southern Christian Leadership Council (SCLC). Other groups believed in confrontation, including the Nation of Islam, the Organization of Afro-American Unity, the Black Nationalist Movement, and the Black Panthers. The Nation of Islam taught that the black race was superior to the white race and that whites were inherently evil and must be totally separated from blacks.

Sex and the Single Girl

In retrospect, it's not surprising that the hippie movement sprang up. America had gone through some very strange times, first with World War I, then the insanity of the Roaring Twenties, then the Depression, and then World War II. Finally, in the fifties and sixties, there was prosperity like the country hadn't seen in quite some time, and material wealth was at an all-time high. But there was also the threat of nuclear bombs.

Women were expected to be mothers and wives first and women second. Their worth was often judged in terms of how happy their husbands and kids were. But it wasn't easy. Women were told to be involved in their children's lives but not to smother their sons for fear of turning them into homosexuals. If women paid too little attention to their kids, they were told the kids would turn into criminals. If they paid too much attention, their kids would wind up gay. The television show *Queen for a Day* taught women that housework was their highest calling and that if their lives were miserable and sexless, it was all for the best. At the same time, Elvis Presley appeared on *The Ed Sullivan Show*, thrusting his hips provocatively, inviting women across America to acknowledge their sexual desires even though they couldn't act on them.

And the women who had learned during the war that they could work, that they could participate actively in society, that they could have lives outside the home, were now thrust back into the roles of wife and mother. After having discovered genuine independence and freedom, they were back to the repressed status quo. The newly repressive government, cranking out new enemies and fears every day, tried to renew a parallel sexual repression. After decades of social chaos and after profound freedom during the war, the already repressive American society became even more repressive to try to restore the prewar social order, desperate to find some kind of calm, some kind of safety and predictability, trying to return to the Victorian moral standards of the previous century, putting women back in the home, back in the kitchen, back into chastity belts, and back on repressive pedestals, all of which was, of course, impossible. The genie could not be put back in the bottle. As there had been during other times of social upheaval (like the turn of the century and the Depression), there was real friction between the demands for conformity and conservatism versus the instinctive human need to express oneself, made even worse by the taste of freedom women had gotten while their husbands and boyfriends were off on the battlefield.

Nowhere was the new role of women more evident than in the person of rock and roll's first female superstar, Janis Joplin, a fiercely ambitious, independent, groundbreaking rock artist who rejected old-fashioned definitions of beauty, femininity, sexuality, and gender roles. Joplin represented one of the biggest changes in America—women's independence. When women found out during the war that they could work and make money, they also discovered that this gave them profound independence. They no longer had to get married to survive in the world. They no longer had to have sex with a man they didn't find attractive in exchange for him bringing home a nice, regular salary to pay for food and clothes and shelter. They found, in short, that they didn't *need* men, and as a corollary, that they could *play* with men. Their financial independence brought with it sexual independence. There was no longer a punishment for sexual promiscuity. An affair no longer meant the loss of security. None of this was being talked about yet, but the reality was there. By the early 1960s even something as seemingly trivial as women's role in social dancing had changed, morphing from the ballroom dancing of the fifties, in which a woman needed a man, to the twist in the sixties, in which a woman could dance with herself if she wanted, where independence was the norm, where men were optional.

In 1948, Alfred Kinsey published his world-shattering *Sexual Behavior in the Human Male*, which declared that more than 90 percent of American men had masturbated, more than half had had affairs, 69 percent had used prostitutes, and 39 percent had reached an orgasm with another man. Not surprisingly, his book was an overnight bestseller. Kinsey hadn't *changed* sex in America; he had just told us what we were all doing, especially the things no one talked about. Suddenly, almost overnight, Americans were talking about sex—in detail—over their kitchen tables. Right-wing politicians and religious extremists immediately denounced all this as immoral and shocking and announced that it would mean the end of the family, just as they did about gay marriage in the eighties and nineties. Needless to say, none of these folks were happy when Kinsey published his next book in 1953, *Sexual Behavior in the Human Female*. This study revealed that 33 percent of American women were not virgins when they married, 13 percent had had sex with more than six partners, and 69 percent of unmarried women who'd had premarital sex had no regrets.

Inspired by this new sexual honesty in America and in response to reinforced efforts at sexual repression and demonization, Hugh Hefner published the first issue of *Playboy* in 1953, with a then virtually unknown Marilyn Monroe scantily clad on the cover and naked inside. In 1962, *Harper's Bazaar* published a full-page color ad featuring the famous model Christina Palozzi, completely nude. (Perhaps the powers that be could have tamped all this down a bit had it not been for the explosion of rock and roll that took America by storm in 1954 and the years following.)

Teenagers became more promiscuous than ever but had not learned enough about birth control. Twenty percent of teenage girls who had sex were getting pregnant. But in 1960, the world changed forever with the invention of "the pill," the first oral contraceptive. For the first time, women had control over when they ovulated, which allowed them to enjoy sexual experimentation outside of marriage without the threat of pregnancy. Though condoms and diaphragms already existed, the pill was easy, safe, convenient, and much more effective, and it changed the way women had sex. Within its first six years, five million women began taking the pill. In 1962, Helen Gurley Brown wrote her great subversive sex manifesto, *Sex and the Single Girl*, also a bestseller, which said it was okay to have sex outside of marriage and, even more subversive, that it was okay never to get married at all. Betty Friedan's 1963 book *The Feminine Mystique* persuasively and controversially attacked the myth of the "happy homemaker." In 1966, sex researchers William Masters and Virginia Johnson published *Human Sexual Response.* Until then, many people did not know the function of the clitoris. Masters and Johnson told them (most notably in a 1969 *Playboy* interview), and it changed everything yet again. By the end of the sixties, many states had struck down their adultery and sodomy laws, and eight million women were taking the pill.

But sexual repression wasn't gone yet. Between the mid-1920s and the mid-1960s, fifty thousand gay men were arrested in New York City alone on charges of homosexuality. It wasn't until 1969 (after *Hair* had opened) and the riots at the Stonewall Inn, a New York gay bar, that the modern gay rights movement was born. It's significant that, when *Hair* opened off Broadway two years earlier, it treated homosexuality as a completely normal, acceptable human variation.

Another interesting phenomenon of the 1960s was a sudden renewed interest in the ancient Indian text, the *Kama Sutra*, which became a runaway bestseller. This ancient religious text (mentioned in *Hair's* song "Sodomy"), describing in great detail every possible sexual pleasure and position, was a blatant and joyful rejection of everything our repressed, fanatically Christian nation thought about sexuality. America was a nation born of Puritans, a nation that believed sex was for procreation only. Not for nothing is Christianity based on a God figure—Jesus Christ—who was born without the "stain" of sex. But the *Kama Sutra* preached the joy and natural rightness of sex. It connected sexuality and spirituality in a way that Western religion could not comprehend and in a way that the hippies of the 1960s found revolutionary and revelatory. In the *Kama Sutra*, sex is not about making babies; it's about pleasure and about finding God. This philosophy connected to the deep spirituality that the hippies searched for and found though mind-expanding drugs and other elements of their movement. It's this philosophy that the song "Sodomy" in *Hair* celebrates, partly in humor, but also partly seriously—"Father, why do these words sound so nasty?" the song asks, and the question makes even more sense to us decades later if we know how popular and widely read the *Kama Sutra* was at that time. In stark contrast to the ideas of Christianity, the *Kama Sutra* believed lovemaking was one of sixty-four arts (also including flower arranging, dance, music, etc.) that should be practiced and mastered. The *Kama Sutra* even had a chapter on the joys of biting and scratching. Imagine what middle-class church-going Americans must have thought of that in 1967. In a culture that believed self-imposed sexual repression was a religious and spiritual ideal, in a culture where religious leaders often denied themselves sex for a lifetime, imagine the reaction to an ancient religious text that claimed the way to become one with God was to lose oneself in wild, unfettered sexual pleasure. And imagine how much these ideas must have appealed to young people looking for any way possible to rebel against their elders.

The Big Picture

Looking back with twenty-twenty hindsight, it's easy to see that the movies of the late 1950s and the 1960s were laying the groundwork for *Hair*, to some extent. Of course, the stage and screen have always had a strange relationship, both antagonistic and parasitic. Hollywood in its early days stole from Broadway on a regular basis, even though the movies had essentially killed vaudeville. It was easier than coming up with original material. Over the twentieth century, the movies sometimes took risks that were copied on stage; sometimes exactly the opposite happened. Many of the greatest film dramas and movie musicals were stage productions first. And yet, as these words are being typed, Broadway seems paralyzed without the movies, including recent and current stage versions of films like *Fame, Big, Footloose, Saturday Night Fever, The Producers, The Graduate, Summer of '42, Thoroughly Modern Millie, 42nd Street,* and *Chitty Chitty Bang Bang*.

Though *Hair* was revolutionary in its content, the movies of the sixties were also tackling and breaking taboos, addressing subject matter that would have been unthinkable just a few years earlier. Some of Hollywood's apparent breakthroughs actually began on or off Broadway, like *Raisin in the Sun, The Connection, A Taste of Honey, The Children's Hour, Tea and Sympathy, Marat/Sade,* among others. But Hollywood also produced original films, tackling gay issues in *Victim,* in 1961; and other sexual and gender issues in *Butterfield 8* and *The Apartment,* in 1960, *Tom Jones* and *Lolita,* in 1962, *Repulsion* and *Sex and the Single Girl,* in 1964, *Darling,* in 1965, *Alfie* and *The Killing of Sister George,* in 1966, and *Far from the Madding Crowd* and *A Guide for the Married Man,* in 1967. Mainstream films addressed the alienation of the younger generation in *To Sir with Love,* in 1966,

The Graduate, in 1967, and *Wild in the Streets,* in 1968 (a teenager becomes president by putting LSD in the water in Washington, D.C.); issues of violence in *Hud,* in 1962, *The Wild Angels,* in 1966, *Bonnie and Clyde,* in 1967; the insanity of war in *Dr. Strangelove or How I Learned to Stop Worrying and Love the Bomb,* in 1964, and *Shenandoah,* in 1965; drugs and alcohol in *The Days of Wine and Roses,* in 1962, and *The Trip,* in 1967; and racism in *In the Heat of the Night,* in 1967, and *Guess Who's Coming to Dinner,* in 1968.

Of course, the films about racial issues were being made by rich white men. But only a few short years later, in the early 1970s, a vigorous, angry black cinema—"blaxploitation" pictures—was born that finally dealt head on and unapologetically with black America. "Blaxploitation" arguably saved some of the mainstream Hollywood studios from bankruptcy.

Hollywood had also discovered psychedelica, with *A Hard Day's Night,* in 1964, and *Wild in the Streets* and *Yellow Submarine,* in 1968. One could even argue that Federico Fellini had been working in psychedelic forms.

And though television was a little behind the silver screen, TV also mirrored the unrest in America in the 1960s. TV became political by airing the Kennedy–Nixon presidential debates in 1960, watched by seventy-five million Americans, the largest television audience up to that point in history. In 1964, a new series debuted, *That Was the Week That Was,* the first political satire on prime-time network television. In 1966, *Star Trek* debuted and managed to address dozens of social issues week after week, all disguised as science fiction fantasy. *Star Trek* became the unlikely source of TV's first interracial kiss. Also in 1966, the clearly psychedelic-inspired show *The Monkees* (copied from the Beatles' film *A Hard Day's Night*) debuted, along with the hardest-hitting political satire yet on television, *The Smothers Brothers Comedy Hour,* which has the distinction of being the only TV show ever canceled for its subversive political content. In 1966, both ABC and NBC had weekly shows covering the war in Vietnam, ABC's *Vietnam Weekly Review,* and NBC's *Vietnam Perspective.* In 1967, *Rowan and Martin's Laugh-In* (taking its title from the be-ins and sit-ins across America) debuted and quickly declared itself as the hippest, most sexual, most open, most forthright show ever on TV. Watching the show today, it's astounding to see what they got away with in 1967, many things that would not appear on network television today.

Forget the Sex and Rock and Roll

Drugs figure prominently in *Hair*, but drugs were not a new phe-nomenon in 1967. Many of the most popular drugs being used in the 1960s had long, legitimate histories. People around the world had been smoking marijuana for thousands of years. Evidence of marijuana cultivation reaches back as far as 2737 B.C. China, where it was used as a treatment for rheumatism, malaria, and absent-mindedness, among other things. It was used recreationally as far back as 1000 B.C. India. The Spanish brought pot to America in 1545, and the English arrived with pot in Jamestown in 1611, where it became a major commercial crop, eventually replaced in the American South by cotton. Marijuana was a principal crop at Mount Vernon and a secondary crop at Monticello. It was intended prima-rily for use as hemp rope, but there is some evidence that its culti-vators were aware of its hallucinogenic properties as well.

As far back as 5000 B.C. the Sumerians were using opium, and the Lake Dwellers of Switzerland were eating poppy seeds as far back as 2500 B.C. Greek naturalist Theophrastus wrote about using poppy juice in 300 B.C. The Greeks celebrated the Eleusinian Mysteries—the drinking of a hallucinogenic beverage—for two thousand years before the Christians stopped the practice in the fourth century. Among the drinkers were many of Western civilization's great thinkers: Aristotle, Socrates, Plato, Cicero, Sophocles, and others. In 1525, laudanum, a form of opium, was introduced into the practice of Western medicine. Throughout the world at this time, alcohol and tobacco were consid-ered deadly drugs and the penalty for their possession or use in some countries was execution. English physician Thomas Dover introduced an opium powder in 1762 that became a very popular medicine. In 1800, Napoleon's army returned to France from Egypt and brought hashish and marijuana with them. In the 1880s, the German army issued cocaine to its soldiers to increase their ability to endure fatigue, and Sigmund Freud began treating his own depression with cocaine. In 1894, the Indian Hemp Drug Commission issued a report com-missioned by the British government, which concluded that "there is no evidence of any weight regarding the mental and moral injuries from the moderate use of these drugs." In 1898, heroin was synthe-sized for the first time in Germany. Until 1903, Coca-Cola contained cocaine. All this history makes it harder to argue with a straight face that drugs are incontrovertibly bad.

Interestingly, in 1900 there were far more Americans addicted to drugs than there were in the 1960s or today. Estimates are that two to five percent of the population were drug addicts in 1900. Part of the reason for this is that morphine was used as anesthesia in medical operations and people became addicted to it. The other part of the reason is the prevalence of "patent medicines" in rural America. Traveling salesman coming to small towns and farms sold elixirs and "medicines" that often contained marijuana, cocaine, or opium. Some contained up to fifty percent morphine, which of course made them *very* popular. And very addictive.

Mainstream recreational marijuana use began in the United States at the turn of the last century, courtesy of Mexican immigrants coming across the border to look for work in the American Southwest. But white Americans weren't feeling very welcoming and were looking for excuses for their racist hatred of Mexicans, so rumors began that pot gave these Mexicans superhuman strength and turned them into crazed murderers. Despite the fact that neither assertion was true, these stereotypes would last for decades. Starting in 1914, local laws began popping up criminalizing marijuana— often not so much as a way of controlling pot use as a way of controlling Mexicans. One Texas state senator said on the floor of the senate, "All Mexicans are crazy and this stuff [marijuana] is what makes them crazy." One Montana state legislator said, "Give one of those Mexican beet field workers a couple of puffs on a marijuana cigarette and he thinks he is in the bullring at Barcelona." From 1914 to 1937, twenty-seven states passed antipot laws.

Throughout the "jazz age" of 1920s America, pot use increased among jazz musicians and people in show business. Marijuana clubs, called "tea pads," began springing up in many major American cities. In 1920, the U.S. Department of Agriculture urged American farmers to grow marijuana as a profitable crop. Pot was still legal in most places, but soon, marijuana was lumped together in the minds of the public with serious drugs like heroin and opium and it was placed under the jurisdiction of the U.S. Treasury Department, which in turn created the Federal Bureau of Narcotics (even though most of the drugs under its jurisdiction were not narcotics), headed by prohibitionist Harry J. Anslinger. The war on marijuana had begun.

And yet, marijuana use continued to spread throughout the country. Sailors from the West Indies brought it into Los Angeles. Jazz musicians from New Orleans brought it up the Mississippi into the Midwest. In 1936, Hollywood produced the now comic but seriously intended "scare film," *Reefer Madness*, which perpetuated the myth that pot drove users insane and turned them into crazed killers.

In 1937 President Franklin Roosevelt signed a marijuana tax bill requiring a government stamp in order to sell or distribute pot. The catch was the government refused to issue any stamps, effectively outlawing pot without actually passing a criminal law against it. The U.S. Congress, known for its usual months and months of hearings on a single issue, spent just two hours of hearings on the Marijuana Tax Act of 1937. The primary witness was Anslinger, who said, "Marijuana is an addictive drug which produces in its users insanity, criminality, and death." (In the following years, based on Ansligner's testimony, five high-profile murder cases invoked marijuana use in their pleas of insanity—to great success.) Dr. William Woodward, of the American Medical Association, also testified, saying, "The American Medical Association knows of no evidence that marijuana is a dangerous drug," to which one hapless congressman replied, "Doctor, if you can't say something good about what we are trying to do, why don't you go home?" The next congressman said, "Doctor, if you haven't got something better to say than that, we are sick of hearing you." After the hearings, the U.S. House of Representatives spent exactly a minute and thirty-two seconds in debate before voting to pass the law. The Senate did not debate at all before voting on it. The government then undertook a campaign of massive arrests throughout the country.

That same year, New York City Mayor Fiorello LaGuardia commissioned one of the first scientific studies of marijuana. Six years of studying the drug produced results proving that pot did not cause increased sexual drive, violence, or insanity. Anslinger was furious and destroyed every copy of the report he could get his hands on, while LaGuardia publicly came out for legalizing marijuana. Anslinger made sure no more pot could be (legally) acquired for any other studies.

Anslinger also shifted his focus from ordinary Americans to movie stars, to up the publicity for his antipot campaign. Actor Robert Mitchum, drummer Gene Krupa, and many other celebrities were arrested and their arrests highly publicized. In response, the major Hollywood studios handed control of their films over to Anslinger, who banned any positive messages about pot in any films.

From 1937, when Ansligner's official war on marijuana began, through 1947, the government spent a whopping $270 million fighting marijuana, a drug proven scientifically to be virtually harmless. In 1948 Anslinger went to Congress for money for more drug enforcement agents. When senators asked him who was violating marijuana laws, he replied (and this is a quote), "Musicians. And I don't mean good musicians, I mean jazz musicians." His statement made all the papers, and within three days the Treasury Department received fifteen thousand letters of protest.

Since Anslinger had stopped the availability of pot for scientific studies, it remains a mystery where he got his information when he announced in the early 1950s that marijuana was a direct and inescapable step to heroin addiction. He also declared that Communists were behind the distribution of marijuana in the United States in order to make Americans "weak" and easy to conquer. In the cold war hysteria of the fifties, this campaign was his most successful yet. He convinced President Truman to sign the Briggs Act, which substantially increased penalties for marijuana possession. In 1958, following the lead of other states, Virginia passed a new law requiring a minimum twenty years in jail for marijuana possession, with no parole. At that same time, Virginia law provided for a minimum fifteen years for murder and ten years for rape.

In 1961, Anslinger addressed the United Nations and convinced one hundred countries to sign an international agreement to outlaw marijuana. By 1963, Ansligner's war on marijuana had cost an additional $1.5 billion.

Finally, in 1967, as *Hair* was opening off Broadway and as marijuana use in America was increasing and becoming more mainstream, the federal government finally allowed a few studies of the drug to go forward, for the first time since LaGuardia's study in the thirties. One study estimated that fully one half of the American soldiers in Vietnam were using pot on a regular basis.

Richard Nixon was running for president on a law and order platform, but since most law enforcement was handled by individual states, Nixon decided to focus on a federal "clean up" of the American "drug problem." (Interestingly, in 1968 the American tobacco industry had gross sales of $38 billion, heavily subsidized by the U.S. government, and spent $250 million on advertising.) Once elected, he sent two thousand customs agent to the Mexican border to stop the flow of marijuana into America. His plan was abandoned after three weeks when virtually no pot was found. Instead, Nixon sent more federal money to local law enforcement agencies to stop marijuana on the local level. As more money was spent and laws were changed, some individuals were being sentenced to fifty years in jail for selling less than an ounce of marijuana, even while a study in 1969 reported that eight to twelve million Americans had used pot at least once. From 1964 to 1969, Anslinger and Nixon spent nine billion dollars on the war on marijuana, for a grand total of nearly $11 billion. In 1970 the U.S. Congress reduced penalties for marijuana possession.

As *Hair* still ran on Broadway, Nixon's own National Commission on Marijuana and Drug Abuse recommended legalization of marijuana, but when Nixon heard about their conclusions, he refused to read their report. Instead of following his own commission's recommendation, he created the Drug Enforcement Agency (DEA) to step up the war. In 1971, he declared that drugs were "America's Public Enemy Number One." But the tide was turning. By 1972, local and state antipot laws were beginning to be reversed, and despite opponents' dire predictions, use did not increase. In 1975 presidential hopeful Jimmy Carter came out publicly for decriminalization of marijuana. But he later reversed his position, and the federal government continued to pour money into its war on marijuana. During the Reagan years, first lady Nancy Reagan launched the earnest but arguably nonsensical "Just Say No" campaign, apparently urging American youth to turn off its collective brain rather than make informed decisions. When all was said and done, the total cost to Americans from 1937 to 1998 amounted to a staggering $301.5 billion. And the result of all that money and effort? If the statistics can be believed, fully one half of our nation's college students are, by definition, "criminals." Not to mention that marijuana is being used today for legitimate medical purposes, including reducing the side effects of AIDS and cancer treatments and (quite effectively) treating Tourette's syndrome.

Lucy in the Sky with Diamonds

And then there's LSD. Allen Cohen wrote in his book *Summer of Love*, "Tripping was common in every area of society from the wealthy and politically powerful to the arts, sciences, and the media.

LSD was trendy, exotic, ecstatic, messianic, and dangerous. It promised psychological healing and spiritual transcendence and often delivered."

LSD was the drug that virtually created the 1960s counterculture, jump-starting a national insurrection among college kids, artists, and other "thinkers." Acid—a popular nickname for LSD—even spawned a subgenre of rock called "acid rock," practiced by new bands like the Rolling Stones, Big Brother and the Holding Company (with Janis Joplin), the Grateful Dead, Jimi Hendrix, and Jefferson Airplane. In 1966, the first San Francisco Trips Festival was held, an acid rock, multimedia event built around light shows, rock concerts, and plenty of LSD. It was the birthplace of the "San Francisco Sound." Dance halls in San Francisco supported this new trend with strobe lights, glow paint, psychedelic posters, and giant lava lamps. That same year, the National Association of Broadcasters told all disc jockeys to screen records for hidden drug messages or obscene references.

The word *psychedelic* comes from the Greeks words *psyche* (soul or mind) and *delos* (to reveal). Following the experiments with LSD by the CIA (in their search for agents for biological warfare), it began to be used by west coast psychotherapists. Captivated by Timothy Leary's experiments with LSD's spiritual and mind-expanding properties, author Ken Kesey and his "merry pranksters" went on a psychedelic bus trip, throwing dozens of wild parties overflowing with LSD and introducing thousands of Americans to the drug. Kesey still claims he could only have written his masterpiece, the novel *One Flew Over the Cuckoo's Nest*, with the help of LSD. In fact, he wrote it while working in a psychiatric ward where they administered the drug to mental patients.

LSD became one of the foundations of the hippie movement in the mid-sixties. Timothy Leary published *The Psychedelic Reader* in 1965. Many users found that LSD (and its more natural equivalents like mescaline and peyote) opened their eyes to the beauty of nature and other simple pleasures that they tended to miss in their regular lives (hence the line in the show "our eyes are open"), and it also gave many users an unparalleled spiritual experience, allowing them to explore their own minds and consciousness. It was this new awareness of inner life and natural beauty that turned many people on to the new counterculture, to the ideas of communes, peace and love, folk music, and "Flower Power." The lyric to "Walking in

Space" in *Hair* clearly articulates all that drugs like LSD, mescaline, and peyote meant to the hippies:

> *My body is walking in space.*
> *My soul is in orbit*
> *With God, face to face.*
>
> . . .
>
> *On a rocket to the fourth dimension,*
> *Total self-awareness the intention.*
>
> . . .
>
> *In this dive*
> *We rediscover sensation.*
> *Walking in space*
> *We find the purpose of peace,*
> *The beauty of life*
> *You can no longer hide.*
> *Our eyes are open*
> *Wide, wide, wide.*

But the American mainstream thought this chemical search for spirituality was dangerous. After all, some religious traditions include admonitions not to try to find or look upon the Creator. The climactic moment in *Raiders of the Lost Ark* illustrates the dangers many religions perceive in trying to get "face to face" with God. On the other hand, more than 10 percent of the hymns in the Hindu *Rig Veda*, one of the world's oldest religious texts, praise the value of the hallucinogenic plant Soma. And Mayan shamans used psilocybin mushrooms.

Hallucinogens have been around for thousands of years, and they've been widely used in America since the 1950s. The hippies didn't invent LSD; they just knew how to market it. Aldous Huxley, author of *Brave New World,* first took mescaline in 1953. Cary Grant took LSD more than a hundred times during the fifties under the guidance of a psychiatrist, as a means to understand and control his alcoholism and womanizing. He swore it helped him. Psychiatrists, mostly in California, used LSD quite successfully to treat not just alcoholism and sexual compulsiveness, but also depression, autism, and other problems. Before it was outlawed in 1966, more than forty thousand patients used it under a doctor's care (who knows how many more used it on their own), and over two thousand scientific papers were written about its effectiveness. But *Time* magazine labeled it an "epidemic" in 1966, and the public and the government soon followed suit.

An LSD trip can manifest itself in hundreds of ways, many of which are dramatized in Claude's drug trip in Act II of *Hair*. LSD can trigger feelings of intense awareness and insight, visions of super bright lights and super intense colors, fantasies (good and bad) populated by characters from the tripper's consciousness, heavily altered memories, and visions of the future. The drug tends to break down the tripper's feelings of individuality and ego, often making fellow trippers seem to blend together into a new combined being. The tripper may experience demons and gods, time travel, and personal connections to historical figures. One user, Alice Dee, writing in Charles Hayes' book *Tripping*, said of one LSD experience, "I had no awareness of body or ego or time, only a profound sensation of illumination and the feeling I was in the presence of All That Is, Eternity, God." Of course, the aftermath of a trip can often be heartbreaking and ego busting, sometimes because the tripper suddenly sees with frightening clarity how pointless and false is the life he's living.

In *Tripping*, Hayes lists Stanislav Grof's four levels of the psychedelic experience: the abstract or aesthetic (sensory enhancement); the psychodynamic, biographical, or recollective (in which the user relives emotional memories similar to dreams); the perinatal (the activation of the subconscious mind); and the transpersonal (in which the user transcends time and space). All of these have their parallels in *Hair*'s trip sequence. Exactly like Claude in *Hair*, many hippies took LSD in the sixties to answer fundamental questions about life: What is true, good, and just? What do I owe to the people around me? What is worth living and dying for? As Berger sings in the show, "I'm evolving through the drugs that you put down."

Many historians believe the cultural revolution of the sixties would not have happened if not for LSD. California outlawed it in 1966 and the United States followed suit in 1968, which only added to its social-rebel appeal. Though it was made illegal, its use behind closed doors continued unhampered. The drug had gone underground and its mythic power only increased. Its status as an illegal, "dangerous" drug made it even more attractive and its allure more potent, as illustrated by the lyric, "How dare they try to end this beauty." And really, will anyone ever quell our curiosity about the unknown, our desire to know God, our quest to find The Answers? If people continue to believe drugs may help them in those endeavors—and they *will* continue so to believe—drugs will always be with us.

One of the saddest consequences of the hopelessly failed American war on drugs is that there are no shamans in our culture today, no guides who understand the value of hallucinogens. Our culture groups together and proscribes addictive drugs that can do damage, like cocaine and heroin, and drugs that generally do not do damage, like marijuana and psilocybin, while making legal other addictive drugs like nicotine and alcohol.

Interestingly, the insurrectionists taking LSD and other drugs in the 1960s are now the mainstream figures running our nation's businesses and our government. Bill Clinton, Al Gore, and George W. Bush have all admitted using drugs. In 1968, Marshall McLuhan foretold that "the computer is the LSD of the business world," never imagining how many of us would have computers in our homes today. Thirty-four states now have laws on the books allowing medical uses of marijuana, and the federal Food and Drug Administration has approved clinical trials of LSD, psilocybin mushrooms, DMT, and MDMA (ecstasy). In the ultimate tribute to both Timothy Leary and *Hair*, the song title "Walking in Space" took on new meaning when, after Leary's death in 1996, his ashes were shot into space and now orbit the earth every ninety-six minutes.

Solid as Rock

The other indispensable element of *Hair* is the music. Never before on Broadway had a musical used serious rock music. *Bye Bye Birdie* had parodied rock music in 1960, but it wasn't until *Hair* that mainstream theatre acknowledged rock as a legitimate form of expression. Looking back it seemed inevitable. In 1967, *McCall's* magazine wrote that rock was "the new language of the contemporary state of mind. It contains freedom, participation, energy, love, sexuality, honesty, and rebellion. It scorns convention, pretense, sentimentality, and false patriotism." They could have been talking about *Hair*.

And nothing changed rock music in the sixties more than LSD, inspiring new forms of lyrics and new kinds of music that left behind the insipid sentimentality of the fifties for a whole new rock experience. The rock and roll of the 1950s evolved into just "rock" in the 1960s, the surprising bastard child of the music of Memphis,

Greenwich Village, and Liverpool, and just as it had several diverse roots, it manifested itself in various ways—surf rock, folk rock, coffeehouse rock, San Francisco rock, protest rock, blues rock, soul, head music, acid rock. And just as the Beats made way for the hippies and post–World War II optimism made way for Vietnam cynicism, the sound and shape of popular music in America (and England) changed dramatically. In response to and in rejection of the sticky sweetness of pop songs in the late fifties and early sixties, young audiences turned to a simpler kind of music—folk—which quickly evolved into a new kind of folk/rock hybrid, as practiced by artists like Pete Seeger; the Kingston Trio; Peter, Paul, and Mary; Joan Baez; Bob Dylan; Simon and Garfunkel; and others. This new folk music was not only political, it allowed its audience to *participate* in its intentions. Pop music didn't entirely lose its obsession with young love, but for the first time in America, popular music began to focus intensely on politics and social change. Outrage became as common as lovesickness on the airwaves. Protest songs became common on the pop charts, including "Where Have All the Flowers Gone," "If I Had a Hammer," "Blowin' in the Wind," "The Times They Are a-Changin'," "The Lonesome Death of Hattie Carroll," "For What It's Worth (Stop, Hey, What's That Sound)," and others. Rock and roll in the fifties was goofy and sentimental. Rock in the sixties was pissed off.

And the songs that did still focus on love seemed to deal more than ever before with loneliness, giving voice to the disenfranchised youth of America in songs like Jefferson Airplane's "Somebody to Love," Elvis Presley's "Heartbreak Hotel," the Rolling Stones' "Paint It Black," Bob Dylan's "I Shall Be Released," Barry McGuire's "Eve of Destruction," Buffalo Springfield's "For What It's Worth (Stop, Hey, What's That Sound)," the Beatles' "Eleanor Rigby," "Help," "Yesterday," and "Got to Get You into My Life," and so many others.

Much has been written about the British invasion of American popular music in the early 1960s. During 1963, not one British song made it into the U.S. Top Ten on the pop charts. During 1964, a third of the songs that made it were British. The Beatles dominated the charts like no group that had ever come before, and they brought many other British bands along for the ride. When the Beatles made their American television debut on *The Ed Sullivan Show*, in 1963, there were over fifty thousand requests for tickets, for an auditorium that seated just over seven hundred. About seventy-three million

Americans watched that performance on TV. That month the Beatles had five singles on the Hot 100 chart, something no band had ever done. The Lowell Toy Company was putting out fifteen thousand fake Beatles wigs a day to meet the demand from Beatles-crazed American kids. And yet, when the Rolling Stones appeared on Sullivan's show in 1964, Sullivan was none too happy with their performance. He later said, "I didn't see the group until the day before the broadcast. They were recommended by my scouts in England. I was shocked when I saw them. It took me seventeen years to build this show; I'm not going to have it destroyed in a matter of weeks." In 1965, the Beatles began experimenting with psychedelic "acid rock" for the first time with their album *Rubber Soul*.

For the first time, popular music began to deal overtly with drug use. Psychedelic or "acid" rock—rock music inspired by or recreating the experience of taking LSD—began to evolve, with songs like Jimi Hendrix's "Purple Haze," Simon and Garfunkel's "Hazy Shade of Winter" and "The Sounds of Silence," Jefferson Airplane's "White Rabbit," the Byrds' "Eight Miles High," the Rolling Stones' "Get Off My Cloud" and "Mother's Little Helper," the Beach Boys' "Good Vibrations," the Shondells' "Crystal Blue Persuasion," Donovan's "Mellow Yellow," the Doors' "People Are Strange" and "Light My Fire," and the Beatles' "Strawberry Fields Forever," "I Want to Tell You," "Got to Get You into My Life," "Tomorrow Never Knows," "Paint It Black," "Rain," "She Said She Said," and of course "Lucy in the Sky with Diamonds," among others. Fans of psychedelic rock claimed that if they listened to this music while on LSD they could *see* the sounds as colors. This connecting of different senses, sound and sight in this case, is called *synesthesia*. A few people have this condition normally, in which tastes register as shapes, sounds as colors, and so on. LSD seemed to unlock those mystical connections that may dwell inside us all.

Many musicians in the sixties refused to play unless under the influence of hallucinogens. The Charlatans were one band that frequently played while tripping on LSD. Other psychedelic-oriented bands (mostly in San Francisco) included Jefferson Airplane, the Grateful Dead, Big Bother and the Holding Company, Country Joe and the Fish, Sopwith Camel, Moby Grape, Quicksilver Messenger Service. British bands Cream, Pink Floyd, and Yes later followed in the psychedelic tradition. And radio stations hated it. The songs were getting longer and longer, sometimes cracking five or six minutes, and their lyrics were getting weirder and weirder, crossing over into poetry and metaphor dense enough that radio station owners couldn't always be sure if they were violating their own decency standards by playing any given song.

After repeated acts of censorship by radio station WMCA in New York, and a *Village Voice* column denouncing it, a massive letter writing campaign to the station was organized. Poet Allen Ginsberg wrote, "We are perhaps in an impasse of racial history and spiritual revolution wherein, with electronic networks linking consciousness together, divine lyric statements do emerge from individual souls that move youthful hearts to an understanding deeper than hysteria. It is inhuman and unworthy of record broadcasters to ignore this noble democratic impulse and shy away from moments when the art approaches its archetypal heart and serves as a medium for moral statement." He went on, "Miraculously, intentions and lyrics of popular music have evolved to include true Poetics. At such a stage, business as usual against so-called 'controversial' works of Poetry are not 'neutral' acts, they are aggressive and vile attacks on human liberty and beauty." In 1965, WOR-FM in New York became the first "progressive rock" radio station and experimental, edgy rock found a new home.

Ian MacDonald wrote that the song "Tomorrow Never Knows" had "introduced LSD and Leary's psychedelic revolution to the young of the Western world, becoming one of the most socially influential records the Beatles ever made." The song included lyrics taken from *The Tibetan Book of the Dead,* which, according to Nick Bromell in his book *Tomorrow Never Knows,* Lennon had found in Timothy Leary's book *The Psychedelic Experience* and had tape-recorded to guide him during one of his acid trips.

At no other time in history could a Bob Dylan have sung the lyric, "Everybody must get stoned!" It was in 1964 that Bob Dylan handed the Beatles their first marijuana cigarette. That was also the year Dylan took his first hit of LSD, which changed his music forever; he left behind his folk roots and dove into explorations of electronic rock. In December 1964, the Beatles released the single "I Feel Fine," with the first ever use of electronic feedback, opening the doors for the acid rock revolution. The first big protest rock songs appeared in 1965, by artists like Bob Dylan, Joan Baez, Donovan, and Barry McGuire. Brian Wilson's first LSD trip led to his 1966 groundbreaking art album *Pet Sounds.* In March 1967 Jimi Hendrix released "Purple Haze," cementing the idea of acid rock. Hendrix and others began experimenting with feedback fuzz in their electric guitar playing, purportedly recreating the sensation of LSD filling the brain. Acid rock made use of repetitive melodies, instrumental sounds altered electronically in the studio, distortion, feedback, reverb, echoes, tape delay, overdubbing, and instruments from other cultures, like sitars, gamelans, and Japanese drums, all designed to reproduce the sensation of tripping.

More than any other previous generation, the youth of the 1960s really lived their lives to popular music. It was a philosophical expression and a communal experience more than simply an escape or a soundtrack for social dancing. The questions teenagers were asking were bigger than who to take to the prom; now the questions were about God and war and politics and eternity. John Connick wrote in *Helix*, in 1967:

> You can't really communicate to the outside how a hundred thousand children of Muzak freaks, who in most cases never bother to study or even think about music, are involved in a single art form to the point where they virtually stake their entire sanity on it. Go to a house and someone hands you a joint in front of a record player and it's assumed that you are going to sit for a couple of hours, not talking, hardly moving, *living* to music.

Furthermore, rock music and its creators understood its paradoxical nature—at once both commercial product and social commentary, both entertainment and catalyst for awareness and action. For the first time, popular music had a self-awareness, an irony, that was undeniable. It had an obligation to address not just teen angst and misfired romance but also political issues and social injustices. It was a lot to ask of rock music. Some of the songs of the era rose to the challenge; some did not.

Never before was listening to music while on drugs such a common experience, almost as if the drugs were required, as if they were a necessary key to unlocking the mysteries of Dylan's lyrics or the Beatles' crazy metaphors. There were questions that needed addressing, and much of the rock music of the sixties asked those questions, even if it didn't provide answers. Rock became a public, communal forum in which to formulate and test philosophies, to share fears and uncertainties, and a basis on which to form a new society, a new way of understanding the world. Rock challenged accepted notions of authority, of sexuality, of gender, of right and wrong, of reality and unreality. Rock music said it was okay to ask these questions out loud, to ask whether everything we'd been taught was actually a lie (even if the perpetrators of the lie didn't know they were lying); and that's what made it so deeply terrifying to so many parents. Most important, rock music told teenagers and young adults that they weren't the only ones asking those questions. It legitimized their questions. The burden they felt but couldn't verbalize was given voice in songs like the Band's "The Weight."

Sandy Darlington wrote in the *San Francisco Express Times*, "Week after week, we go inside the music, and as they play and we listen and dance, the questions and ideas slowly germinate in our mind like seeds. . . . The music is more than entertainment. It describes and helps us define a way of life we believe in." The sixties changed forever the way popular music worked. Still today, bands like the Dave Matthews Band and Smashing Pumpkins follow in the footsteps of their sixties precursors, sometimes taking that sound to its next logical step, sometimes stepping back in time to the style and sound—and intentions—of the sixties.

All this came together in the score to *Hair*. Perhaps it was precisely because Galt MacDermot was not a rock composer that he could so artfully explore the various forms of sixties rock in *Hair*, from the rockabilly of "Don't Put It Down" to the "folkie" rock of "Frank Mills" and "What a Piece of Work Is Man" to the rhythm and blues of "Dead End," "Sodomy," "Easy to Be Hard," and "Abie Baby" to the protest rock of "Ain't Got No" and "The Flesh Failures" to the acid rock of "Aquarius," "Three-Five-Zero-Zero," and "Walking in Space" to the mainstream pop of "Good Morning Starshine."

3 Growing *Hair*

The Great Off–White Way

Though most Americans weren't aware of it, nowhere was American life changing more than in New York theatre. Perhaps the greatest revolution in the history of American theatre happened in the 1950s and 1960s, and it led directly to the creation of *Hair*.

It all started in 1952. The phenomenon we now know as off Broadway theatre had begun a few years earlier in small ways, but in 1952, a revival of the Tennessee Williams play *Summer and Smoke* at Circle in the Square became the first major New York theatrical success outside the Broadway theatre district in thirty years. The *New York Times* had sent critic Brooks Atkinson to review the show, much to everyone's amazement; the *Times* had never reviewed an off Broadway show before. And when his rave appeared in the paper the next day, off Broadway was off and running, finally a legitimate and commercially viable alternative to the slick shallowness of much of Broadway's product.

Unlike Broadway, where the bottom line was always profit—no matter what noble artistic intentions went along with that—off Broadway was a place where new actors, directors, and playwrights could get their work seen, where shows that hadn't worked on

Broadway could be given a second look, where theatres could become institutions, nurturing work and artists over time and developing loyal audiences, rather than being just real estate, a place to rent to do a show. Producer Joseph Papp brought to the off Broadway community the idea of creating a safe environment in which to experiment, to risk, to break the rules, without the pressure of commercial success hanging over the enterprise. The emphasis was on the work, the creation process, more than on box office success. Julian Beck and Judith Malina brought to off Broadway an intellectual point of view. Off Broadway also became one of the most fertile grounds for work in improvisation.

Off Broadway had begun, in a sense, back at the turn of the century, but it was then more about idealistic amateurs than serious theatre professionals. And World War II put an end to that experiment. Until 1952. Off Broadway brought back to life the idea of staging a show with the audience on three sides of the stage, or in some cases all around the stage. That's how theatre was always done centuries ago, but the modern standard had become the impersonal proscenium arch, separating audience from actors by a stage frame, footlights, and often an orchestra. After hundreds of years, actors and audiences were coming back together. Off Broadway was an adventure, an experience not encountered on Broadway in a very long time. Many off Broadway theatres were even in questionable neighborhoods, adding to the adventure.

Off Broadway companies like Circle in the Square became the launching pad for many of the greatest actors in America, names like Geraldine Page, Colleen Dewhurst, George C. Scott, George Segal, Dustin Hoffman, and innumerable others. Off Broadway was where American theatre learned to cast against type, to refuse to pigeonhole talented actors by the work they had done in the past or the roles they "looked" like they should play. In fact, off Broadway repeatedly took giant leaps that Broadway copied only years later. Off Broadway was the first place audiences saw plays dealing with African American self-identity and drug addiction. Off Broadway led the way back to the kind of heavily polemical, psychological, political plays and topical revues Broadway had done so well in the 1930s.

In 1959, *Variety* reported that investment in off Broadway shows for the first time totaled one million dollars. There were now more than thirty off Broadway theatres where there had been only a handful just a few years earlier. The *New Yorker* assigned a special critic just for off Broadway shows. And a number of off Broadway shows went on national tours for the first time. The following year, the landmark experimental musical *The Fantasticks* opened off Broadway. (It remains to this day the longest-running musical in the world.) By this time, there were twice as many shows opening off Broadway each season as there were on Broadway.

Also in 1959, the otherwise lightweight off Broadway musical *Once upon a Mattress* became one of the first New York shows to practice colorblind casting, putting Jane White, an African American actress, in the role of the Queen—playing mother to the Caucasian actor Joe Bova. In 1961, Jean Genet's off Broadway play *The Blacks* caused a sensation, addressing issues of race and racism in the most radical, most relevant terms ever on a New York stage. The show ran for more than 1,400 performances and it signaled the birth of black theatre in America. In 1962, the play *Alarums and Excursions* satirized growing American involvement in Vietnam for the first time. In the fall of 1962, the Writers' Stage, a new off Broadway theatre company, was born, and its founders wrote a statement of purpose:

> In an age when mankind has developed the means to annihilate itself, the problems of the individual are only important in their relationship to and in reflection of the major problems of our day, moral, political, social, atomic. We would like our theatre and our audience to ask themselves collectively what our theatre has to do with Survival, Peace, Sobel, Chessman, or the movement to the far right.

Experimental Theatre and the Roots of *Hair*

Off off Broadway, which really had yet to be discovered by the public, was home to New York's most radical experimental theatre movement. Off off Broadway artists tried to stay small, to ignore reviews, to resist commercial pressures and temptations, and concentrate entirely on the work. In the middle and late sixties, when *Hair* was created, this movement had been going on for quite some time, led by directors like Joseph Chaikin, Peter Brook, Jerzy Grotowski, and Antonin Artaud; writers like Samuel Beckett, Jean Genet, and Eugene Ionesco; companies like the Living Theatre, the Group Theatre, and the Open Theatre; and theatre spaces like Joe Cino's

Caffé Cino, and Ellen Stewart's La MaMa Experimental Theatre Club. Theatre works during this time were based heavily on improvisation, on group creation, on ritual, on exploring new ways to communicate with an audience and new ways to involve an audience directly in the act of performance. The creation process, often by way of extended workshops, was as important—or, in some cases, more important—than the presentation of the work.

Off off Broadway practitioners rejected the conventional notions of director, playwright, script, rehearsal, and character. They saw great significance in the fact that the word *playwright* ended with *wright* instead of *write*; in other words, they believed that the job of a playwright is not just to write down dialogue but instead to fashion a play, in the broadest possible sense, from other materials, to be a "metamorphosing collagist." In fact, the idea of scripts written down on paper and frozen in form held little import for these theatre innovators. Richard Schechner, in his introduction to the published script of *Viet Rock*, wrote that "performance, action, and event are the key terms of our theatre—and these terms are not literary."

The Living Theatre was founded in 1947 by expressionist painter Julian Beck and his wife, Judith Malina, who had been a protégé of the famed European experimental director Erwin Piscator. Beck had gone to Yale, dropped out, enrolled at City College of New York, then dropped out again, a philosophical anarchist who counted Gandhi and Thoreau as his moral guides. Malina was the daughter of a German actress and had been born in a theatre in Germany. Beck and Malina's theatrical guide was the great director Antonin Artaud. In his book, *The Theater and Its Double*, Artaud wrote:

> We can begin to form an idea of culture, an idea that is first of all a protest. . . . A protest against the idea of culture as distinct from life—as if there were culture on one side and life on the other, as if true culture were not a refined means of understanding and exercising life.

The Living Theatre was begun as a conscious alternative to commercial theatre, focusing in the 1950s on staging unconventional poetic dramas by writers like Gertrude Stein, Jean Cocteau, Garcia Lorca, and Bertolt Brecht. Their work used ritual, audience participation, nudity, and other experimental devices, and it drew upon various mystical and contemporary sources, including, in addition to the work of Artaud, the ancient Kabbalah philosophy and the frequent use of LSD. Their shows often encouraged audiences to chant, smoke marijuana, take their clothes off, even engage in sexual acts during performances. Julian Beck once explained, "We were willing to experiment with anything that would set the mind free. We were practicing anarchists, and we were talking about freedom in whatever zones it could be acquired. If drug trips were a way of unbinding the mind, we were eager to experiment." Another time Beck said, "LSD carried with it a certain messianic vision, a certain understanding of the meaning of freedom, of the meaning of the as yet unattainable but nevertheless to be obtained erotic fantasy, political fantasy, social fantasy—a sense of oneness, a sense of goodness, a marvelous return to the Garden of Eden morality." Members of the Living Theatre were often arrested during political protests, sit-ins, and peace marches. They didn't just talk and write about politics; they engaged themselves actively in the issues of their times.

The Living Theater achieved international fame when in 1959 they staged *The Connection*, a "jazz play" about drug addiction. There was no curtain. Its documentary style aimed at complete audience involvement because all the action appeared to be happening in real time. The play was reportedly uncomfortably real for audience members, some of whom became ill watching it. The local daily critics all hated the show, while most of the foreign critics loved it. Walter Kerr wrote in New York's *Herald Tribune*, "I have a feeling that the distrust of art, because art may distort the truth, may in the end leave us with very little to hold in our hands." Critics were ill equipped to review this new kind of theatre intelligently. Applying the standards of old-fashioned musical comedy, the roles of audience and artists, traditional linear narrative, to this radically new kind of theatre caused most critics to miss the social significance and deeper intentions of these new works.

Perhaps predictably, the Living Theatre was considered dangerous and, as with the controversial political theatre works of the 1930s, the Living Theatre's various New York venues were shut down by the government—though not officially for being controversial. In 1953, the New York City Fire Department closed down the group's Cherry Lane Theatre for fire code violations. In 1956, the Living Theatre Studio was closed by the city's Building Department for building code violations. All while other theatres in similar venues went untouched. (Even as recently as 1992, a new Living

Theatre venue was closed down for building code violations.) The company itself was closed down in 1963 by the I.R.S. for back taxes, and the Becks were indicted in 1964 for impeding Federal officers and failure to pay taxes. So, for the rest of the sixties, the company became nomadic, touring their shows throughout Europe and living as a collective, focusing more and more on using theatre as a tool for social change. In the 1970s, the Living Theatre began performing their socially conscious work in nontraditional venues, including prisons in Brazil, slums in Palermo, steel mills in Pittsburgh, and New York City schools. In the 1980s, they developed new participatory techniques in which audiences would rehearse with the group and then join them onstage for performances. The company's mission (in part) was

> to call into question who we are to each other in the social environment of the theatre, to undo the knots that lead to misery, to spread ourselves across the public's table like platters at a banquet, to set ourselves in motion like a vortex that pulls the spectator into action, to fire the body's secret engines, to pass through the prism and come out a rainbow . . . to move from the theatre to the street and from the street to the theatre.

Joe Cino's Caffé Cino is often (and incorrectly) called the birthplace of the off off Broadway theatre, operating from 1958 to 1968 and producing the early works of some of America's great theatre artists—Lanford Wilson, Sam Shepard, Marshall W. Mason, Robert Patrick, Jean-Claude van Itallie, Tom Eyen, William M. Hoffman, and others. The historical impact of Cino's coffeehouse began early on, as Cino encouraged artists to hang their work on his walls and encouraged poets to read their poetry for patrons. Poetry readings led to readings of plays, which led to staged readings, which led to actual (though small) productions. Later on, Cino focused more exclusively on one-act plays. The works he presented, on a modest eight-foot-square stage, included new plays and classics, experimental works and more traditional pieces, even musicals—and many of the pieces were gay themed. The actors used the kitchen as a dressing room (imagine how sanitary that was). Several of the shows that debuted at Caffé Cino went on to successful off Broadway runs (including the musical *Dames at Sea,* which introduced the world to Bernadette Peters), and Mason and Wilson went on to form New York's prestigious Circle Repertory Theatre. Cino refused to read scripts submitted to him. If a playwright wanted a production, Cino gave him one. There was no admission charged, just a basket passed. There was no pressure to make money, no pressure to get good reviews, no pressure to run long or get big crowds, since neither was possible here. It was a radical idea in 1960—free theatre that was just about art. But Actors Equity (the professional actors union) and the New York Police Department didn't like theatre going on in coffeehouses (where it couldn't be regulated), so the police frequently showed up, either passing out summonses or actually shutting down performances.

In 1961 composer and clergyman Al Carmines became the assistant minister at Judson Memorial Church, in downtown New York, near Washington Square Park (across the street from where *Hair's* Jeanie would someday meet Frank Mills in front of the Waverly Theatre). Carmines soon opened the Judson Poets' Theater, dedicated to experimental theatre forms, especially those involving music, and Carmines composed the scores for many of the shows that ran there. Small shows were produced in the choir loft; bigger shows and musicals were produced in the main sanctuary. In response to controversy and criticism over the work being done by Judson Poets' Theater, Carmines said:

> God can take care of himself. This is the first article of Judeo-Christian religion: we don't have to protect God. We don't create God. We can do a decadent play or a cynical play that's totally nihilistic, with the feeling that we can be exposed to it without secret weapons—without having to think in some way in your mind of defending yourself.

La MaMa E.T.C. opened its doors in 1961 at Ellen Stewart's Café La MaMa. It was one of the shining lights of experimental theatre in the 1960s and one of the first venues to house resident companies, including the La MaMa Troupe, led by Tom O'Horgan (who later directed *Hair*); Mabou Mines, led by Lee Breuer; and a couple dozen others. La MaMa publicly declared itself "dedicated to the playwright and all forms of the theatre." In 1965, the La MaMa companies went on the first of many European tours, to Paris, Denmark, Sweden, and other countries. In 1966, La MaMa "moved up" from off off Broadway to off Broadway, as Circle in the Square produced an evening called *Six from La MaMa*. Later on, in 1971, La MaMa provided the debut of the musical *Godspell*, a piece following many of the structural precedents of *Hair* but much lighter in tone and presentation. It was so successful it was moved to a Broadway house. And La MaMa is still thriving today with three theatre spaces, a gallery, and other arts resources.

In 1963, after four years with the Living Theatre, Joseph Chaikin left to form the Open Theatre, dedicated to "opening the minds of actors and audiences," and he both acted and directed with the group. His interest was less in politics and more in artistry, in finding a stronger method for actors to approach nonnaturalistic, experimental work. He rejected naturalistic, or "method," acting because he believed the emphasis on re-creating reality kept an actor from exploring meaning beyond the surface. He developed a very confrontational, very improvisational style of theatre that clearly had its roots in the work of the Living Theatre but was also a radical departure. He wrote that the goal of the Open Theatre was "to redefine the limits of the stage experience, or unfix them, to find ways of reaching each other and the audience." The group's process usually began with a playwright suggesting a form or idea, often inspired by previous improvisational work by actors; then the actors would take this jumping-off place, improvise some more, and expand the idea. Eventually—whenever they felt they were ready—the piece would be written down, though rarely fixed in "permanent" form. Paul Sills, who would go on to found the Second City improvisation company in Chicago, worked with the Open Theatre for a time and built his work on theirs. One of the Open Theatre's directors, Peter Feldman, described their work this way: "Whatever realities are established at the beginning are destroyed after a few minutes and replaced by others. Then these are in turn destroyed and replaced. These changes occur *swiftly* and *almost without transition*, until the audience's dependence upon any fixed reality is called into question." (This method of creating theatre was later used in *Hair*, as members of the tribe continually transformed into other characters and situations with virtually no conventional transition.) Among the Open Theatre's works were Samuel Beckett's *Endgame*, Jean-Claude van Itallie's *The Serpent* and *Interview*, and Megan Terry's groundbreaking *Viet Rock*. Several of the Open Theatre's plays went on to off Broadway productions, including *American Hurrah* and *Viet Rock*. The Open Theatre disbanded in 1973.

Also about that time, Richard Schechner formed the Performance Group, a company interested in experimenting with physical space, involving the audience more fully in the theatre experience by moving the performance into the audience's space or by moving the audience into the performance space. Producing shows at the Performance Garage, they worked with scaffolding, multilevel platforms, ramps, and bridges, running in and out of the audience space. With audience members usually sitting within inches of playing areas, the result was a greatly heightened intensity on every level; what was once tragic became nearly unbearable, what was funny became hilarious, and what was public and dramatic became highly personal, private, and intimate. Schechner received great praise for many of his shows, including *Dionysus in 69*, *Makbeth*, and *Commune*. He wrote in the *New York Times*, "Theater is an unliterary art, a here and now experience. Its finest expressions are immediate, gestural, involved, inclusive, and participatory."

In 1964, Broadway producer Richard Barr, who had moved almost entirely to off Broadway theatre, introduced absurdist theatre to America via Beckett's *Happy Days* and *Play*, Pinter's *The Lover*, LeRoi Jones' *The Dutchman*, as well as plays by Ionesco, Genet, and other writers. Theatre of the Absurd addressed important social issues by exaggerating and twisting the facts to the point of absurdity. It raised questions without offering answers.

The 1966–67 season saw some of the angriest theatre yet open off Broadway, plays about disillusionment, about America falling down on the job, about pressing social and political issues. The time was ripe for a show like *Hair*. In 1966, the nastiest political satire ever seen, *MacBird!*, posited a fictional Robert Kennedy taking revenge on President Johnson for the murder of his brother. And off Broadway was experimenting with nudity. In 1967, the *New York Times* lamented "neither the best season nor the worst, but the barest."

All of these groups, artists, and shows planted the seeds that came to fruition in *Hair*. Off off Broadway was a place of artistic discovery and no judgment. Artists considered the process more important than the end product. It was never a lesser theatre or a tryout for off and on Broadway. It was a separate theatre tradition with all-new rules and all-new possibilities. The artists of off off Broadway wanted to renew American theatre, go back to the basics, start over from scratch. Broadway and even off Broadway had strayed from the path of pure art, or so the artists of off off Broadway believed. They were determined to change things.

Hair coauthor Jerry Ragni was one of the early members of the Open Theatre. He had worked both in experimental theatre and in more mainstream work, having appeared off Broadway in *The Knack, War,* and *Hang Down Your Head and Die,* and on Broadway, in 1964, in *Hamlet* with Richard Burton, directed by John Gielgud. Coauthor Jim Rado had acted and written several musicals and revues in college, hoping early on to become a traditional mainstream musical theatre composer. He studied method acting with renowned teacher Lee Strasberg (of the Group Theatre) and eventually appeared on Broadway in *Marathon '33, Generation,* and *The Lion in Winter.* Rado also appeared off Broadway in *Hang Down Your Head and Die,* where he met Ragni. It was Ragni who turned Rado on to the amazing possibilities only beginning to emerge within the burgeoning experimental theatre movement.

Composer Galt MacDermot had been born in Montreal but went to college at Capetown University, in South Africa. He brought this African influence to the music of *Hair,* using the rhythms of the rituals of the Bantu tribe, the driving pulse of African music, and the habit of musically setting stresses on unexpected syllables (as in "What a Piece of Work Is Man," "Ain't Got No Grass," and other *Hair* songs), a stylistic device only recently becoming mainstream in rap and hip-hop. In a 1969 interview, MacDermot described the music he heard in South Africa. "They'd be playing what was really rock and roll. What they called *quaylas*—like a South African version of High Life—very characteristic beat, very similar to rock. Much deeper, though, much more to it. It's just got a *fantastic* feel to it. Africans, when they get a beat going, it's just something." He went on, "Everything I write is sort of influenced by that, of course. *Hair* is very African—a lot of rhythms, not the tunes so much. . . . It's a long time now, but my feeling for the music, what I learned in Africa, I still remember." MacDermot went on to write three more Broadway shows, two flops, *Dude* and *Via Galactica,* and one hit, *Two Gentlemen of Verona.* MacDermot also composed a number of film scores and music for a few plays. He continued to add music to *Hair* over the years.

As an example of just how far ahead of his time MacDermot was, many of his compositions are now being used as raw material for contemporary hip-hop artists, in tracks as diverse as Busta Rhymes' "Woo-Hah!! Got You All in Check," Run-DMC's "Down with the King," Quasimodo's "Loop Digga" and "Discipline 99," the Beatnuts' "Uncivilized," Handsome Boy Modeling School's "The Truth," Rah

Digga's "Lessons of Today," and Thirstin Howl III's "Brooklyn Hard Rock." MacDermot is thrilled. He was quoted recently in the *Village Voice* as saying, "It's great that my stuff is being picked up by these hip-hoppers, 'cause those guys are allowing rhythm to come back. Disco kinda killed rhythm for a while there in the seventies, and rap brought it back. To me, that's what music's all about."

Hair director Tom O'Horgan was directly involved in the experimental theatre movement, most notably at La MaMa E.T.C., and after *Hair*, would go on to bring that philosophy to the Broadway production of *Jesus Christ Superstar* as well. About the controversy over *Hair*, he said in a 1968 *Newsweek* interview, "Obviously it means something if people are bothered." The *Newsweek* article called O'Horgan's brand of theatre "sensual, savage, and thoroughly musical," and went on to say, "O'Horgan disintegrates linear, verbal structure and often breaks up and distributes narrative and even character among different actors. . . . He enjoys sensory bombardment." Describing his creative process, the article said, "O'Horgan's method is extreme permissiveness based on exploratory improvisations with his actors." O'Horgan began writing operas at age ten, and in third grade began to create (but never finished) a marionette performance of Wagner's *Ring* cycle. While at DePaul University he became interested in twelve-tone music. He learned to play dozens of musical instruments, collected ancient and rare instruments from various cultures, and even had a kind of neo-vaudevillian, absurdist harp-playing act he performed at coffeehouses. He worked with the famous improvisation company Second City, for which he wrote scores for many performances. He wrote plays, operas, and lots of other music before becoming a director, but often acted as both director and composer, for shows like *Lenny* and *The Tempest*. He worked at Caffé Cino, Judson Church, and elsewhere throughout the late 1950s and early 1960s. He worked at Café La MaMa from 1961 to 1968, both directing and composing. After *Hair*, he went on to direct many plays in London and elsewhere in Europe, and later on Broadway he directed *Jesus Christ Superstar, Dude, Inner City, Sgt. Pepper's Lonely Hearts Club Band, The Leaf People*, and others. Of *Superstar*, critic John Simon wrote, "The entire production looks rather like a Radio City Music Hall show into whose producers' and designers' coffee cups the gofer had slipped some LSD."

In a piece for the *New York Times* in 1969, O'Horgan wrote, "It seems obvious to everyone except those most vitally concerned with Broadway's welfare that any peace demonstration or rock concert has more actual theater and audience than ninety percent of the boredom perpetrated on Broadway." He went on to predict doom for the commercial theatre. "Theater will not die. It will just move elsewhere, and, if we assiduously apply the methods we have been using, Broadway will become a parking lot full of cars with no place to go." Some today would argue that it has become just that.

Viet Rock

The fact that Ragni was working on Megan Terry's play *Viet Rock* was certainly a major factor in the development of *Hair* and in the development of Ragni and Rado as writers. Had Ragni not been working on this seminal—though sadly forgotten—work of experimental theatre, there's little doubt *Hair* would have turned out differently. Critic Richard Schechner said, "the theme and scope, the variety and density of *Viet Rock* would have excited Brecht." In the *Village Voice*, Michael Smith wrote, "*Viet Rock*, vividly expressed, is a breakthrough . . . extraordinary on at least two counts. It is the first realized theatrical statement about the Vietnam war . . . and a rare instance of theater confronting issues broader than individual psychology."

These theatrical values certainly found their way into *Hair*. The reviewer for *Variety* called it "wild . . . an acid indictment . . . ensemble acting effects that have to be seen to be believed . . . *Viet Rock* has been brilliantly staged. These Open Theater types are contributing something new to the concept and technique of stagecraft." Al McConaghan, of the *Minneapolis Tribune*, anticipated what the critics would later write about *Hair* when he wrote, "*Viet Rock* is more important than what it means . . . it is an original and gutsy bit of theatre. It is a theatrical demonstration that . . . ambushes an audience with an extraordinary evening of theater and . . . it wins as an emotional gut shot at the tragedy of the times."

Viet Rock was a play partly written, partly group devised through improvisation in rehearsal, a practice already widely used in the experimental theatre community. The famous director Gordon Craig argued that it was very likely that Shakespeare used the same method, that he lifted story ideas from other works and from English history, brought them to his company of actors, and let them improvise scenes. A secretary wrote down what happened, and Shakespeare took this home to rework, polish, and convert into iambic pentameter. Though there's no way to know if that actually happened, it makes sense. Shakespeare accomplished something in his plays no other writer had ever done up to that point—incorporated distinctly realistic and complicated psychology, relationships, and interconnected plot threads. He brought real life onto the stage in an unprecedented fashion, giving different characters remarkably different verbal patterns and linguistic gestures, and explored the interconnectivity of human lives more interestingly than anyone else had. Though there's no doubt as to his genius with words, it isn't impossible to believe the beautiful complexity of his work came from the input of more than one mind.

While it's true that playwright Megan Terry is no Shakespeare, she achieved, to a lesser extent, many of the things that made Shakespeare's work special, painting on an epic canvas the great human events of birth, death, war, love, and loss. She used both low and high comedy, tragedy, satire, parody, music, dialogue and monologue, mime, and poetry.

Called the mother of American feminist drama, Terry's process was fascinating. Each play began as an idea, filtered through extensive improvisation by company members, then solidified into a text. But the text was hardly a finished product. Her plays continued to evolve as they were performed, sometimes *over*evolving, achieving a kind of balance and artistry, then losing it as change continued. As with *Hair*, even after the script of *Viet Rock* was published, in 1967, subsequent productions did not feel the necessity of sticking slavishly to the text. Each production was a source of rediscovery and reconstruction. Also, because of this creation process, the end result rarely had the kind of structure and logic to which mainstream theatre seemed shackled. And because of its improvisational roots, *Viet Rock*—much like *Hair*—was full of pop culture references to movies, commercials, political slogans, TV shows, and yes, Shakespeare.

Instead of each scene following logically from the one before, the scenes in *Viet Rock* (and also in *Hair*) were connected in other ways, in what director Richard Schechner called "prelogical ways." A scene could connect to the previous scene psychologically. It could go off on a tangent from the scene before. It could further explore or compress the previous scene. It could act as counterpoint or could stop the action dead to explore mood or relationship. The connection between two scenes might be nothing more than the free association that comes from improvisation.

In fact, *Viet Rock* opened this way, with the actors coming onto the stage at the beginning and lying down. As a song played, the actors became a human, primordial flower, newborn infants and their mothers, naked army inductees and doctors, and then those same inductees and their mothers.

These scenes or "action-blocs" (Terry's term) could, in many cases, be rearranged without damaging the show. In fact, many of the scenes in *Hair* were rearranged when the show moved from off Broadway to Broadway. This rearranging changed the show, changed its focus, but it didn't cause the show to crumble as it would have with most plays. But it's important to note that those connections, those transformations from one moment to the next, were not random or accidental. They were the work of a playwright at the height of her power, knowing what to use and what to throw away, knowing how to weave a complex tapestry whose accumulated power is undeniable, working in a new form that may have been misunderstood but was no less legitimate than what was happening in the commercial theatre of Broadway.

One of the devices of this theatre movement was to divorce the actors from the characters. The director or playwright would have the actors swap roles in the middle of the show, or even in the middle of a scene—not just to confuse the audience, as many have suggested, but to force the audience to stop connecting on a merely emotional level and actually think about *what* is happening. Instead of watching the actors, the audience now watches the action. This was a theatre of ideas, not characters, and the breaking of an audience's long-held theatregoing habits wasn't easy. In Megan Terry's much praised play *Keep Tightly Closed*, three actors portrayed three characters in a jail cell, all linked by a murder. One man hired the second to hire the third to kill the first man's wife. But to focus the audience's attention on the actions and themes of the story instead of on the individuals, Terry had the three actors continually shift among the three characters throughout the play; in a few scenes, one of the actors even became the murdered wife as the murder was reenacted.

Terry used this device in *Viet Rock*, in the senate-hearing scene, as actors continually replaced each other, swapping positions as senators, witnesses, and observers. In her stage direction, Terry wrote: "The actors should take turns being senators and witnesses; the transformations should be abrupt and total. When the actor is finished with one character he becomes another, or just an actor."

Of course, some audience members just couldn't handle this weirdness—and even today, a lot of people can't handle such things in shows like *Hair*. They dismiss these experiments as "chaos" or as "arrogance" or a conscious disdain for the audience. It's none of those things. It's merely the discarding of old-fashioned rules to get an audience to watch a performance in a different way, to reach an audience in a different way, to accomplish something new.

Viet Rock aggressively confronted its audience with an angry antiwar message. In one scene, a group of women chanted "U.S. Government Inspected Male!" (a variation of a phrase that pops up in *Hair* as well) as their men passed physicals to the tune of "Stick 'em in the arm, stick 'em in the end!" The *New York Times* described part of the show like this:

> After the girls have made themselves into an outlined airplane and flown future heroes to the jungles where the napalm burns, they drop to their knees for more choral unison: "Citizens arrest! Make love, not war!" They get robot replies in return. If they have battered out a rhythmic "Innocent people are being burned!" they get a short, snappy, automated "Gee, we are sorry about that" back from the boys.
>
> A boy crawling on his belly lifts his head for a split second to intone, "I can't wait till I get there and make a killing on the black market!" Three Vietnamese women, moving their mouths in soundless spasms of anguish, are waved away loftily by a ladylike voice: "Usher, please escort these ladies to the powder room. I think they'd like to freshen up." Uniformed lads on a three-day spree in Saigon accompany their dancing with fiercely inflected slogans: "Let's go gay with L.B.J.! I got syphilis today because of L.B.J.!"

The acting style rejected conventional naturalistic acting or dialogue. The text rejected plot and linear structure. In a bit of comic artistic self-reference that doubled as political comment, a politician in one scene declares, "This administration, of which I am a part of, indulges in anything but realism."

The way Megan Terry and the Open Theatre created *Viet Rock* was a blueprint for many who came after, involving the actors in shaping a work for performance, expanding the American musical comedy form to include rock music, borrowing clichés of the mass media, and having the actors leave the performance space to interact with the audience. Ragni was a part of this process, adding to the piece along with the other actors, and he brought all these techniques with him to *Hair*.

In a way, *Hair* used all the tricks and techniques of *Viet Rock* but did it better—or perhaps more accurately, did it more accessibly and more commercially. But we can't ignore one of the great truths of theatre: innovation doesn't matter if the show isn't successful. *Pal Joey* made many of the same great innovations as *Oklahoma!* and did it three years earlier. But *Joey* was a flop and *Oklahoma!* was a monster hit. Nobody copied *Pal Joey*. Everybody copied *Oklahoma!* If *Joey* hadn't been revived in the 1950s, with greater success, nobody would even remember it. Similarly, *Viet Rock* was a landmark theatre piece in many ways, but hidden away downtown at Café La MaMa, nobody knew about it. Uptown, on Broadway, everybody knew about *Hair*, so *Hair* got all the credit. This is not to say that Ragni, Rado, MacDermot, and O'Horgan did not all bring enormous original contributions to *Hair*, but it's important to remember that *Hair* did not leap fully grown from the ether. It had roots in the rich, fascinating theatre going on downtown, a theatre in which most of *Hair*'s creators were involved.

Hair brought so much from the experimental theatre movement, most notably the idea of theatre as ritual. The show's opening number, "Aquarius," is a ritual summoning of the tribe, a formal calling together of the members of this group of hippies. In the original Broadway production, when the song began, the hippies were out mingling with the audience. They froze and then began moving to the stage in slow motion, coming together on stage in a large circle, a potent symbol of life that would be used throughout the show, a mystic form that was borrowed directly from the opening of *Viet Rock*. Ritual is used in many moments in the show, in the mock Catholic mass of "Sodomy," in the be-in, in the passing of the joints before the trip, in the marching and chanting that happen throughout.

Many other devices in *Hair* can also be found in *Viet Rock*—actors becoming children; the use of nudity; references to other American wars; references to soldiers' serial numbers; specific antiwar chants from the 1960s; a scene of parachuting from a helicopter (along with surrealistic comments as the soldiers float to earth); the use of gongs and other Asian instruments; references to the *Kama Sutra*; an orgy scene; depictions of murder; soldiers crawling on their bellies through the jungle; references to "the red man and the yellow man," the Madonna, and Jesus Christ; a Buddhist priest; the use of incense and slow motion; references to LBJ, the Pope, and Shakespeare.

Another area the experimental theatre movement was exploring was the idea of words as sounds, as percussion, or as background noise, divorced from literal meaning, something Gertrude Stein had played with earlier in the century. In the senate-hearing scene in *Viet Rock*, one witness' monologue devolved into surrealistic percussion-speech:

> . . . the ignorant and sensational press just has to blow everything up. Blow it up. Blow it up. Blow it up. Blow it up. Bleep it. Blop. Bleep, gleep, blow. Sleep, sleep, sleep. Forgive me, but I haven't had any sleep in eighteen months. Blow it up. Blup. Blup.

Similarly, in songs in *Hair* like "Ain't Got No Grass," "Three-Five-Zero-Zero," and "The Bed," words come at the audience like a freight train, so fast, so quirky, that no audience could ever catch it all or comprehend it all. But these lyrics aren't intended just to be comprehended; they are to be enjoyed as abstract sounds. Toward the end of "Ain't Got No Grass," the lyric deconstructs itself into a list of words and phrases based on the sound "pop." The words don't make complete sense; they have become percussion. They are no longer meaningful words; they are just sounds. *Hair* was the first impressionist Broadway musical, in which lyrics, dialogue, plot, and character were often not drawn conventionally—they were implied, suggested, abstract. As the impressionist painters created only the impression of form and structure, to be interpreted and synthesized by the eye and mind, so *Hair* did with the art of theatre.

Give My Regards to Concept Musicals

Despite the obvious evidence, we have to be careful in suggesting that *Hair*'s stage roots lie *only* off and off off Broadway. Though nothing like *Hair* had ever been produced on Broadway before, the Broadway musical had been evolving, and there is a clear path toward the convention-shattering *Hair*. The bigger question is, have we continued to follow the path *Hair* laid out for us?

The term "concept musical" would not be coined until several years after *Hair* opened, but that doesn't mean concept musicals didn't already exist. Today, the term gets bandied about with a great deal of casualness, and there are as many definitions as there are people using it. Shows as diverse as *Company, Pippin, Assassins,* and *A Chorus Line* have all been called concept musicals, and yet the term does have its uses. Most shows labeled as concept musicals do have elements and purposes in common, and they essentially fall into four categories:

- Musicals built on a central concept, usually an important social issue, instead of a linear story (the "pure" concept musicals).
- Musicals whose central concept is most important but that still employ a linear plot.
- Character studies with no linear plot but no unifying concept either.
- Musicals that don't really fit into any other categories.

There have not been very many shows that have completely discarded traditional linear plot in favor of a central, unifying concept, probably because these musicals usually do not do very well financially. They are hard to write because there is no easy, logical framework on which to hang the songs and characters; the songs and scenes can be in practically any order and still make a certain amount of sense. These shows are harder for audiences to understand: without a story, the audience must discern for themselves what the show is about, and without a conflict to resolve there is no traditional emotional payoff at the end. (Since *Hair* does have a minimal plot and a substantial emotional through-line, it doesn't have those problems.)

The first concept musicals on Broadway were both "pure" concept musicals focusing on a single concept—Marc Blitzstein's satire *The Cradle Will Rock,* in 1937, and *Love Life,* in 1948, with music by Kurt Weill, book and lyrics by Alan Jay Lerner. *The Cradle Will Rock* was a very funny, very disturbing, very political, episodic, nonlinear musical, told mostly in flashbacks, that explored the various ways in which our capitalistic society tried to squash the burgeoning labor unions. It was the first American musical from a working-class perspective. It laid the groundwork, in its politics, its aggressive, angry satire, and its episodic construction, for later shows as varied as *Cabaret, Hair, Pippin, Chicago, Assassins,* and *Rent.* It enjoyed a healthy run in New York, and has become one of the most performed, most revived, most recorded of all Broadway musicals. *Love Life* was a surrealistic musical that followed a married couple through one hundred and fifty years of American history, using the marriage and its growing cynicism as a metaphor for the birth and growth of the country. The show was billed as a "vaudeville" (as *Chicago* was in 1975), and used vaudeville-style songs placed outside the action, breaking the fourth wall, to comment on the action. Weill had developed this device in his work with Bertolt Brecht on *The Threepenny Opera* and other shows. *Love Life* has very little linear plot or development, only interconnected vignettes tracing the nonaging couple and their two children from 1791 to the present. As life in America becomes more complex, the family members begin to experience a strain on their relationships. Robert Coleman in the *Daily Mirror* called it "an exciting study of the rise, demise, and rebirth of standards." Though Coleman loved it, other critics found it depressing, cold, hard to understand, and hostile to its audience (accusations also thrown at *Company* in 1970). It ran only 252 performances.

Hair, Company, and *Assassins* also fall into the category of "pure" concept musicals, in which linear storytelling is mostly discarded in favor of exploring one central idea—the 1960s counterculture in *Hair*, the difficulty of long-term emotional commitment in modern America in *Company*, political assassination as the underbelly of the American Dream in *Assassins*. But almost no other New York musicals have been created in this mold. The few "pure" concept musicals fall so far apart historically (1937, 1948, 1967, 1970, and 1990) that it may be quite some time before the experiment is repeated.

The second category of concept musicals includes shows whose central concept is the most important element despite having a traditional linear plot. These shows can be seen as either concept musicals that hedge their bets or conventional musicals with a gimmick. The first Broadway musical in this category was *Cabaret,* in 1966, just a year before *Hair* opened at the Public Theatre, and it is no accident that its director, Harold Prince, also directed and helped conceive *Company* four years later. Perhaps *Cabaret* was Prince's practice run at creating a concept musical. It was the first such musical since *Love Life,* but this time the show was a hybrid of traditional book musical and concept musical. The scenes in the Kit Kat Klub seemed to be part of a nonlinear, thematically developed "pure" concept musical. In these scenes, performers broke the fourth wall (or more accurately, pulled the audience *inside* the fourth wall), there was very little dialogue, and the songs were commentary songs *about* the action rather than a part of it. But the scenes *outside* the club belonged in a traditional book show. These scenes had naturalistic dialogue, an intact fourth wall, and traditional, integrated songs. Perhaps the commercial failure of *Love Life* prompted the *Cabaret* team to hedge their bets by giving their audience the best of both worlds, although *Love Life's* brief run makes us wonder if *Cabaret's* creators had even seen it. Only later, in Bob Fosse's film version, were the integrated book songs cut and the show converted into a "pure" concept musical. The revivals of *Cabaret* in the 1990s moved the show more fully into the category of "concept musical."

In 1967, *Hallelujah, Baby!* opened on Broadway just a few months before *Hair* opened off Broadway. Following in the footsteps of *Love Life*, it tells the story of a young black woman who does not age from the turn of the century to the present. Her life is a metaphor for race relations in America, but instead of mere vignettes exploring these themes, her story does follow a (somewhat) linear plot and employs (somewhat) integrated book songs. Like *Hair*, it explores issues of racism and black civil rights, sometimes through very pointed satire. Other shows in this category include *Pippin, Chicago, Nine, Grand Hotel,* and *The Will Rogers Follies*. These shows all dip their toes in the waters of experimentation, some further than others, but none really jumps in.

The third category, musical character studies with no linear plot or single unifying concept, are fewer in number but include shows like *Jacques Brel Is Alive and Well and Living in Paris, A Chorus Line, Working,* and *Songs for a New World*. Still, some have suggested that *Jacques Brel* and *Songs for a New World* are a category unto themselves—abstract musicals.

The last category of concept musicals includes those musicals that do not fit into any other category; we call them concept musicals for lack of a better label. Not surprisingly, most of these genre-busting musicals are Sondheim shows. *Merrily We Roll Along* is a traditional book musical, except the book runs backward. *Follies* is mostly a character study yet it has a central concept as well as a minimal plot. *Pacific Overtures* has a linear plot but is told through the conventions of Kabuki theatre, dispensing with many western storytelling devices.

We have to keep asking the questions that *The Cradle Will Rock*, *Love Life*, *Hair*, *Company*, and *Assassins* have asked. Does a musical have to have a linear plot? Are there other ways to tell a story? Why must scenes follow in a "logical" sequence? Can we not tell a story out of chronological order (as *Pulp Fiction* did)? Do scenes have to end with songs as the Rodgers and Hammerstein school taught us? Must a show provide a clear resolution or answer at the end of the evening, or can it ask more questions? And further, what can we learn about communicating stories, issues, and concepts from TV, movies, music videos, talk radio, modern dance, performance art, improvisation, and of course, cyberspace? How can we follow developing technology's lead and make musical theatre truly interactive? Conversely, can we shed all the trappings of technology and go back to the basics of the empty stage? Did *Hair* teach us some important lessons that we ignored? Is it still just as revolutionary and convention shattering as it was in 1967, for the simple reason that we didn't learn its lessons and carry its experiments forward?

In 1928, Jerome Kern and Oscar Hammerstein turned musical theatre upside down by shattering accepted rules in *Show Boat*. In 1943, Rodgers and Hammerstein began a major new trend in serious book musicals with *Oklahoma!* After sixty years of the Rodgers and Hammerstein model, might it be worthwhile to go back and reconsider the innovations of *Hair* and see what we have to learn from them? Right now, a new generation of musical theatre writers from coast to coast is ready to break more rules and find new ways to take this uniquely American art form and its audiences into the future. Maybe *Hair*, even though it was written way back in 1967, is the guidebook they're looking for.

4 Evolution of the Revolution

Downtown

Hair was chosen to open Joseph Papp's Public Theatre, the new indoor theatre space for his New York Shakespeare Festival. *Hair* originated in a workshop Jerry Ragni conducted at the Open Theatre. While Ragni was acting in the Open Theatre's *Viet Rock* at Yale University, and while Papp was teaching there, Ragni presented Papp with an early draft of his and Rado's American tribal love-rock musical. Papp thought it was deeply flawed but loved its spirit and its intentions. He agreed to produce it, after some more work was done on it.

Interestingly, neither Ragni nor Rado were hippies (and only two of the original Broadway cast members were); but the authors found the hippie counterculture fascinating, and once they decided to write *Hair*, they spent all their time in Greenwich Village with the hippies, doing research. Off Broadway producer Eric Blau (who would go on to create the cult hit musical *Jacques Brel Is Alive and Well and Living in Paris*) introduced Ragni and Rado to composer Galt MacDermot, who agreed to set their bizarre and wonderful lyrics to music. Blau became the show's first producer, but when Papp guaranteed an eight-week run at the Public Theatre, Blau encouraged

Rado and Ragni to take the offer; Blau could only guarantee an opening, no more.

Then Tom O'Horgan entered the picture. Almost. Jim Rado says, "Gerry and I discovered Tom O'Horgan directing a play called *Futz* by Rochelle Owens at the Café La MaMa. We wanted Tom to direct *Hair* at the Public Theatre, but he was booked to tour his La MaMa troupe in Europe and was unavailable. He was gone for a few months during which time our show was cast, rehearsed, and had its six-week run at the Public." The show opened in October 1967, under the direction of Gerald Freedman and with a top ticket price of $2.50. It was the perfect time for *Hair*.

The original off Broadway production started off with the song "Red, Blue, and White" (later renamed "Don't Put It Down"), emphasizing the stronger focus on the Vietnam war in the show's first version. Interestingly, this song was sung by the "adults" at the Public, though it was given to the tribe members on Broadway. The most shocking thing for people who know only the Broadway version is that at the Public, the song "Aquarius" didn't appear until two-thirds of the way through Act II. And the show ended with "Exanaplanetooch" and "The Climax." Also interesting are the differing amounts of music—only nine songs in Act I at the Public, but *nineteen* in Act I on Broadway (of course several of these songs were unusually short). Act II also changed during the move, but the number of songs stayed constant. There is an early published version (now out of print) that people often think is the off Broadway script, but in fact it's not. It's a strange hybrid of the off Broadway script and various changes the authors were contemplating before they set about making wholesale changes for the Broadway production. That script, as published, was never performed.

The song list off Broadway was:

ACT I

"Red, White, and Blue"
"Ain't Got No"
"I Got Life"
"Air"
"Going Down"
"Hair"
"Dead End"
"Frank Mills"
"Where Do I Go?"

Act II

"Electric Blues"
"Easy to Be Hard"
"Manchester, England"
"White Boys"
"Black Boys"
"Walking in Space"
"Aquarius"
"Good Morning Starshine"
"Exanaplanetooch"
"The Climax"

Uptown

After the original eight-week run ended at the Public Theatre, Ragni and Rado busily rewrote and expanded the text, and they wanted a more experimental director to take the show forward. Though Gerald Freedman and the choreographer Anna Sokolow had done a decent job of getting *Hair* off the ground, the authors felt Tom O'Horgan, who was now back in New York, could be the pilot to take it soaring into the next dimension. Papp and independent producer Michael Butler moved the show to the Cheetah, a New York disco located on Broadway in the theatre district, but because the Cheetah was still an operating disco, *Hair* had to start at 7:00 P.M. and play without an intermission in order to clear the place in time for the disco crowd. Butler wanted to move the Papp/Freedman production directly to Broadway from the Cheetah, but Papp didn't think it would work on Broadway and so pulled out. According to Jim Rado, he and Ragni confronted Michael Butler with their ideas about the new script and the thirteen new songs, about recasting and re-rehearsing the show from scratch, with Tom O'Horgan at the helm. At first Butler turned down these proposals. He loved the Cheetah show and wanted to move it intact. Ragni, Rado, and MacDermot walked away from that meeting and started looking for a new producer. A week later they received a call from Butler agreeing to hire O'Horgan and produce the new *Hair* with the new script.

So, with massive revisions and new songs, new cast members, a new director, a new choreographer (they wanted the movement to look more spontaneous, less "choreographed"), and the addition of designers Jules Fisher and Robin Wagner, Michael Butler moved the new and improved *Hair* to Broadway's Biltmore Theatre. Previews began on April 11, 1968, and the show opened on April 29. Butler's astrologer picked the opening date to ensure a successful run.

While the show was in rehearsal, at Ukrainian Hall, in the East Village, the producers were having trouble finding a Broadway theatre that wanted it. Various people came downtown to see rehearsals, and just in time a Mr. Cogan appeared, an independent owner, offering the Biltmore. The authors went to look at the theater. Rado sat in the front row and suggested a raked stage, the first for a Broadway musical, and that raked stage became a dramatic element in Robin Wagner's dynamic, impressionistic set.

Butler may well have been the perfect person to produce *Hair*. Not only did he have the money to treat the show right, he had once been an adviser on Indian and Middle Eastern affairs to President Kennedy, and he had run for public office. Once Kennedy was assassinated, Butler dropped out of politics. Until *Hair* came along. In 1967, he sampled pot for the first time and soon reversed his prowar stance on Vietnam. Though he first went to see *Hair* thinking it was about Native Americans, he soon discovered it was really an antiwar rant, very much in keeping with his newfound political leanings, and he was determined to get involved. In 1969, after *Hair* had settled into its Broadway run, Butler told the Chicago press corps that the musical represented a new kind of communication between "the young idealists and the great uncommitted semi-establishment people."

In addition to all the personnel changes that took place after the run at the Cheetah, the show's authors kept rewriting the script and drastically changing the score. "The Climax" was cut. "Dead End" was cut (and restored and cut and restored throughout *Hair*'s life). And "Exanaplanetooch" and a song called "You Are Standing on My Bed" were still in the show in previews but cut before it opened. In fact, several changes were made soon after the Broadway opening, including the addition of "I Believe in Love." Thirteen new songs altogether were added for Broadway, a few of which had been written for the Public version but not used. Some original cast members say the song "The Bed" was cut and restored over and over again after the Broadway opening, but Jim Rado says it was always in the Broadway production. The song "What a Piece of Work Is Man" was written during rehearsals for Broadway. This speech from *Hamlet* had been spoken by Claude at the Public, and MacDermot now turned it into a song. The *Hamlet* moment, now sung by two tribe members, was also moved slightly, from after the trip to inside the trip. MacDermot loved taking dialogue and setting it to music. The song "Hashish" came from an early speech of Berger's, and the song "Nineteen Thirties" (also known as "Hello There") came from a speech that Claude delivers to the audience. Jeanie's monologue about the how much she "digs" Claude was turned into a song called "I Dig," but though the authors were very happy with it, the song never made it into the show. Lincoln's Gettysburg Address in the show became a song for the movie version of *Hair*, though it didn't make it into the final cut. More recently, MacDermot has greatly musicalized portions of Claude's trip that had not been musical before. (This habit is not surprising, since MacDermot has said he always wanted to write rock operas.) In the end, the song list on Broadway was:

ACT I

"Aquarius"
"Donna"
"Hashish"
"Sodomy"
"I'm Black"/"Colored Spade"
"Manchester, England"
"Ain't Got No"
"I Believe in Love"
"Air"
"Initials"
"I Got Life"
"Going Down"
"Hair"
"My Conviction"
"Easy to Be Hard"
"Don't Put It Down"
"Frank Mills"
"The Be-In"
"Where Do I Go?"

ACT II

"Electric Blues"
"Black Boys"
"White Boys"

"Walking in Space"
"Abie Baby"
"Three-Five-Zero-Zero"
"Good Morning Starshine"
"The Bed"
"Aquarius" (reprise)
"Manchester, England" (reprise)
"Eyes Look Your Last"
"The Flesh Failures"/"Let the Sun Shine In"

When *Hair* began its national tour, censorship reared its ugly head. In Boston, in 1970, the district attorney tried to shut *Hair* down for "lewd and lascivious" content. The case went quickly to the state supreme court, which ruled that *Hair* constituted legally protected protest speech, and that it could go on, but only if all cast members remained clothed "to a reasonable extent" and "all simulation of sexual intercourse or deviation" was eliminated. The cast refused to alter the show's content and shut it down themselves in protest. The president of Actors Equity Association, Theodore Bikel (Captain Von Trapp in *The Sound of Music* on Broadway) sent a letter of support to the *Hair* cast, forcefully denouncing censorship. The case went on to the U.S. Supreme Court, which did not clear the way for *Hair* to open without threat of legal action. In St. Paul, Minnesota, a clergyman trying to shut down *Hair* released eighteen white mice into the lobby in hopes of frightening the audience. No one noticed.

As new productions were launched in cities across America, young people by the thousands came to audition, to become a part of the significant event that is *Hair*. In San Francisco, in 1969, eighteen hundred people showed up to audition. The first day of auditions in Chicago that year saw twenty-two hundred hopefuls, and the total came close to four thousand. Meanwhile, hundreds of kids kept auditioning for replacement spots in the Broadway cast.

Return to *Hair*

Hair was revived on Broadway in 1977 but closed after only seventy-nine previews and forty-three regular performances. New pop culture references were added, to Andrea McArdle (star of Broadway's *Annie* at the time), to Crazy Eddie and the Reverend Sun

Myung Moon. Songs like "Exanaplanetooch" went in and out of the show on a regular basis, the script and score still not fixed in any permanent form. But in 1977, *Hair* existed in some kind of temporal limbo, not a period piece quite yet, nor really contemporary either. Today, the show can be played as a period piece and its emotional impact is profound, but perhaps in 1977 the hippie movement was still too recent to be history but not current enough to feel relevant. Whatever the reasons, the revival flopped.

In the *New York Times*, Richard Eder wrote, "Nothing ages worse than graffiti. [*Hair's*] message—liberation, joy, pot and multiform sex, the vision of youth as a social class of its own and, in short, the notion that there can be flowers without stalks, roots, or muck to grow in—has faded. It is too far gone to be timely; too recently gone to be history or even nostalgia. . . . It falls, or rather, it sags. Its virtues remain, but ten years after its first appearance they look much feebler than they must have seemed at the time. Its glow is forced; its warmth become sentimentality and worse, sententiousness. Over and over one is reminded of the worst kind of religious art: the simpering or soulful hippies recall the simpering plaster Virgins and soulful Christs sold around shrines."

In *Newsweek*, Jack Kroll wrote, "You can't go home again, as Thomas Wolfe said, and you can't grow *Hair* again, as seems clear from the Broadway revival of the 1967 sensation that at least dented the chrome trim of the American musical theater. Right away, when the cast in their tribal regalia fans out into the theater, declaring their love for the members of the audience, you don't believe it. They're perfectly nice kids, doing a gig, but for some reason you don't love them back. A lot has happened in the decade since *Hair* first blew in our eyes, and the Revelation According to St. Hippie is both too close chronologically and too distant emotionally to work now."

In the late 1980s, Ragni, Rado, and MacDermot revised *Hair* in some substantial ways, adding "The Vietnam Song," and "Hippie Life." Still later, in the 1990s, MacDermot created an extended "War" musical sequence.

On Screen

Ragni and Rado wrote a screen treatment for the proposed film version of *Hair*, but Czechoslovakian director Milos Forman didn't like it. He didn't want a film version so close to the stage version. He wanted a more conventional story. So a linear plot was conceived for the film and a new screenplay written by Michael Weller, who also wrote the screenplay for *Ragtime*, another film heavily criticized for not doing justice to its source. Claude was removed from the tribe and reimagined as a young man from Oklahoma coming to New York to enlist in the army. Berger and the tribe befriend Claude and they have their adventures. Still, despite the new plot, the basic relationships remain—Claude is still in love with Sheila, who is still in love with Berger. Sheila is no longer a member of the tribe, but her character only partly changes; she is still a college girl who is fascinated by Berger and the tribe, though here she lives in the suburbs with her parents and has no interest in social issues. Claude still trips in the film, but his ingestion of LSD is almost random instead of at the hand of Berger, and the subject of his trip is his love for Sheila, not his fear of going to war. Also, in the stage version, Claude trips on natural hallucinogens—mescaline and peyote—not on the man-made chemical LSD. The biggest change of the film is that Berger is the one who dies in Vietnam, not Claude, through a ridiculous mistaken-identity plot twist, shifting the emotional focus of the story but not until pretty late in the game.

The problem with trying to graft the existing score onto a new, linear storyline is that the songs often fit the action very badly. "Manchester" comes out of the blue, for no logical reason whatsoever. "Walking in Space," a song about preparations for doing illegal drugs in secret and the effects of those drugs, is set inexplicably against a montage of Claude in basic training. The section of the song about the bright colors a tripper sees on LSD accompanies scenes of violence and hardship in basic training. It's as if the screenwriter and director had no idea what the song is about.

Maybe *Hair* shouldn't have been a movie; maybe its experience needs to be live and visceral. Or maybe there was a way for *Hair* to be filmed without being so greatly altered. Still, the movie has its fans, and many people come to know and love *Hair* the stage show through *Hair* the movie.

The score changed a great deal in the movie as well. The two versions of "Ain't Got No" from the stage version were combined. Several songs were recorded for the soundtrack but not used in the final cut of the film, including "Abie Baby," "Air," "My Conviction," "Frank Mills," and "What a Piece of Work Is Man." The fact that these songs made it onto the soundtrack probably means they were intended to be used in the film; it's interesting to guess where they might've gone in that very different script. The funky Gettysburg Address from the Broadway production, spoken with back-up singing, was fully musicalized for the film, and though it didn't make it into the final cut either, it was preserved on the soundtrack as "Fourscore." The musical fragment "Hello There" and the song "Don't Put It Down" both became underscoring. "I Believe In Love," "Going Down," and "The Bed" were all cut outright. The songs in the film are:

"Aquarius"
"Sodomy"
"Donna"
"Hashish"
"Colored Spade"
"Manchester, England"
"I'm Black"/"Ain't Got No"/"Ain't Got No" (reprise)
"Party Music" (instrumental, based on "Hello There")
"I Got Life"
"Hair"
"LBJ"
"Electric Blues"
"Hare Krishna (The Be-In)"
"Where Do I Go?"
"Black Boys"
"White Boys"
"Walking in Space"
"Easy to Be Hard"
"Three-Five-Zero-Zero"
"Good Morning Starshine"
"Somebody to Love" (as background music only)
"Don't Put It Down" (instrumental only)
"The Flesh Failures"/"Let the Sun Shine In"

The movie met with mixed reactions, but Vincent Canby, in the *New York Times*, called it "a good, authentically stylish movie musical."

Authenticity

Maybe later stage productions and the film version of *Hair* failed in certain ways because of a lack of authenticity. Certainly, in the rock community in the fifties and even more so in the sixties, authenticity seemed of paramount importance. Quality, polish, musicianship, often seemed to be of less value to fans than emotional and personal truth. Rock artists and especially folk rock artists were judged on how "real" they were in their work, how personal the work was, how genuine their performances seemed. Performers like Janis Joplin and Jimi Hendrix delivered authenticity. Rightly or wrongly, when Bob Dylan's work morphed from folk rock to acid rock, his fans were outraged because they believed electrics distanced his performance, robbed it of its authenticity, changed it into manufactured art instead of pure, personal folk art. Throughout history, any time electricity has come between performer and audience, outrage has resulted. The same thing happened when amplification first came to Broadway. In almost every case, after a while, the objection fades.

So, yes, maybe *Hair*'s later problems did have to do with an authenticity issue. Real or imagined, the first *Hair* (both off and on Broadway) seemed to exude a kind of authenticity that few Broadway musicals ever had. Interviews with cast members at the time and later on confirm that the actors believed what the show preached, believed in the peace movement, believed in the hippie culture, believed in the value of sexual freedom, the use of mind-expanding drugs, the search for existential meaning outside mainstream religion. Sometimes they came into *Hair* already believing in those things; sometimes *Hair* changed what they believed. Some of the actors even went onstage stoned from time to time, lending *real* authenticity to their performance. And we shouldn't forget that the guys who wrote the show took the two leading roles, lending even more authenticity to the show. Ragni and Rado were expressing their own thoughts and beliefs onstage, the words they had written, even if some of those beliefs originated in a hippie culture of which they had not initially been a part. In so many ways, *Hair* was Real, and audiences knew it.

But reconstructing that "reality" a decade later, then twenty or thirty years later, with the same team may have been impossible. The show was built on authenticity, and one could argue that authenticity cannot, by its very definition, be re-created. *Daily Variety* reviewed a Los Angeles staged concert version of *Hair* in 2001, writing, "The production misses out on something fundamental. *Hair* was a 'happening,' highly influenced by Julian Beck and Judith Malina's Living Theater, which was thriving at the time. The show didn't just depict a 'be-in,' it *was* one, taking advantage of the the-ater's essential presentness to create an experience, something more than a show." Still, there are productions today around the world and across the United States that do create that authenticity, that do connect to audiences in much the same way as the original, produc-tions in which the actors—the tribe—do genuinely believe in what they're saying, in the messages that *Hair* proclaims.

Maybe it's just that *Hair* must be discovered fresh each time for it to really work. Several Broadway musical revivals in the last decade were profound and unexpected revelations for audi-ences—*Carousel, Cabaret, The King and I, Oklahoma!*, and others. And almost all these revivals were directed by non-American directors. Some have theorized that Americans knew these works too well, that we were unable to come at them fresh, that we couldn't step back and see them the way they were seen when they were new. But foreign directors, who had not grown up with the movie versions and repeated community theatre productions, really could see these great works freshly. Maybe *Hair's* creators were the wrong ones to mount subsequent productions of *Hair*. Maybe the men who made *Hair* in its original form, who made it so real, so immediate, so fresh, could never recreate that authen-ticity. Maybe it takes new people, maybe even people who didn't live through the sixties in America, people for whom the sixties are a new experience, a revelation, a wondrous new landscape in which to explore and discover all the mysteries and complexities that fed into the genius of *Hair*. Maybe truly authentic produc-tions of *Hair* now require of their creative teams the same explo-ration and discovery, the same innocence that informed the original.

Across the Atlantic Sea

Hair was not just an American phenomenon. There were many for-eign productions of the show, and luckily there are many foreign cast albums of *Hair*, several of which have been released on CD, most of which contain an interesting mix of English and foreign lyrics. There are cast albums on LP or CD from Australia, Brazil, Copenhagen, France, Germany, Hungary, Israel, Italy, Japan, London, Mexico, and Sweden.

There was also an RCA album called *DisinHAIRited*, containing twenty songs written at one time or another as part of the *Hair* score. Seven of the songs were used in the Broadway production but couldn't fit on the original LP cast album. Most of the other songs on the album never saw the light of stage performance, though "The Thousand-Year-Old Man" and "So Sing the Children on the Avenue" were both used in a production in Toronto, directed by Ragni and Rado. *DisinHAIRited* is out of print, but it may soon be available on CD. The album includes:

> "The Thousand-Year-Old Man"
> "So Sing the Children of the Avenue"
> "Manhattan Beggar
> "Sheila Franklin"/"Reading the Writing"
> "Washing the World"
> "Exanaplanetooch"
> "Hello There"
> "Mr. Berger"
> "I'm Hung"
> "The Climax"
> "Electric Blues"
> "I Dig"
> "Going Down"
> "You Are Standing on My Bed"
> "The Bed"
> "Mess O' Dirt"
> "Dead End"
> "Oh Great God of Power"
> "Eyes Look Your Last"/"Sentimental Ending"

Jim Rado added some of these songs to the show over the years, and the latest version of Hair includes "Dead End," "Sheila Franklin," "Hello There," "Oh Great God of Power," and "The Bed."

Crossing Over

Since the beginning, pop artists have recorded the songs of *Hair*, sometimes topping the pop charts. The Fifth Dimension's recording of a medley of "Aquarius" and "Let the Sun Shine In" made it to number one on Billboard's pop charts in 1969, followed in the number two spot by the Cowsills' "Hair" and in the number three spot by pop star Oliver's "Good Morning Starshine." That same year, Quincy Jones recorded "Dead End" and "Walking in Space." Nina Simone recorded a medley of "Ain't Got No" and "I Got Life" in 1968 and performed it many times over the years. Three Dog Night and Shirley Bassey both recorded "Easy to Be Hard." "Aquarius" has been recorded by the Everly Brothers, Johnny Mathis, Engelbert Humperdinck, and many others. Barbra Streisand recorded "Frank Mills"; as recently as 1993, so did the Lemonheads. Even more recently, songs from *Hair* have been sampled into rap songs like "C'mon Wit da Git Down" by the Artifacts, Run-DMC's "Down with the King, and "Old to the New" by Nice and Smooth. And that's just the tip of the iceberg: hundreds more recordings have been made of the songs from the show.

Hair Extensions

All three of *Hair*'s authors went on to write other projects directly or indirectly linked to *Hair*. The first opened in the summer and fall of 1971, the other three opened in the fall of 1972.

In the spring of 1971, composer Galt MacDermot began working on a multiracial rock musical version of Shakespeare's *Two Gentlemen of Verona*, with lyrics by playwright John Guare and a book by Mel Shapiro. Building on many of the themes in *Hair*, MacDermot and his collaborators returned to linear storytelling, though not without putting their own distinguishing mark on Shakespeare's original. The musical opened at the New York Shakespeare Festival's Delacorte Theater in the summer of 1971 and that fall moved across town and received nine Tony nominations, winning two, for best musical and best book. Clive Barnes wrote of the off Broadway production, in the *New York Times*, "The New York Shakespeare Festival Public Theater is currently doing Shakespeare a power of good and turning Central Park into a place of celebration with its new production of *Two Gentlemen of Verona*. It is *jeu d'espirit*, a bardic spree, a midsummer night's jest, a merriment of lovers, a gallimaufry of styles, and a gas. It takes off." After its move to Broadway, Barnes wrote, "It has a surge of youth to it, at times an almost carnal intimation of sexuality, and a boisterous sense of love. It is precisely this that the new musical catches and makes its own.

The musical also has a strange New York feel to it—in the music, a mixture of rock, lyricism, and Caribbean patter, in Mr. Guare's spare, at times even abrasive lyrics, in the story itself of small-town kids and big-town love. It also has a very New York sense of irreverence. It is a graffito written across a classic play, but the graffito has an insolent sense of style, and the classic play can still be clearly glimpsed underneath." This was the only one of the post-*Hair* projects to succeed.

In October of 1972, Gerry Ragni and Galt MacDermot's rock musical *Dude* opened at the Broadway Theatre, and it ran a mere sixteen performances and lost a reported $800,000. According to some sources, Ragni had been making random notes for the show for several years and had amassed two thousand pages of them, which somehow found their way into fifty songs. The production team gutted the Broadway Theatre, to create an in-the-round performance space that was "landscaped" into mountains, valleys, and forests. The band was deployed in several areas throughout the space, and microphones for the actors were hanging and hidden everywhere. Actors climbed all over the theatre and were raised and lowered on various wires. The ground was at first covered with dirt, but when that caused too much dust, it was sprayed with water and became mud. Finally it was replaced with shredded army blankets. Traditional seating areas were renamed the valleys (orchestra seats), foothills (mezzanine), mountains (balcony), and other whimsical and ultimately confusing labels, which just made for grumpy ticket sellers and buyers. After the third preview, the director was fired and Tom O'Horgan was brought in to reshape the show while it was shut down for three weeks. It reopened in only slightly more coherent shape. Still, the score was recorded and makes for a generally satisfying concept album.

Clive Barnes wrote in the *Times*, "In *Hair* the very aimlessness of the piece, its random poetry and shafts of insight could afford the luxury of a nonstructure because it was describing a lifestyle that deliberately embraced nonstructured patterns as its aim. *Dude*, on the other hand, seems to be an allegory about 'that great theater in the sky,' and an allegory that is not clear, even on its primary level, is in no end of trouble." Richard Watts wrote in the *Post*, "I at least gathered that the narrative had to do with good, evil, the need for love, and the conflict between constructive and destructive urges in mankind. But the way in which it goes about making its points struck me as being more bewildering than illuminating." Douglas Watt in the *Daily News* wrote, "*Dude* is a boisterous, sprawling, unfocussed entertainment—a kind of half-baked allegory—bent on telling us in the broadest theatrical terms about growing pains, about life and love and the joy in simple pleasures. What it winds up as is an overblown recital of a few dozen songs, some of them pleasant, by Galt MacDermot (music) and Gerome Ragni (book and lyrics), two of the writers of *Hair*. Call this Son of *Hair* and too big for its britches."

In November that same year, MacDermot opened yet another rock musical, *Via Galactica*, a space fantasy with lyrics by Christopher Gore and Judith Ross, directed by the noted British director Peter Hall. The set consisted of six large trampolines, which were used to convey weightlessness, along with lots of smoke, lasers, and a flying spaceship. The hero of the piece, Gabriel Finn, was a space garbage man battling the depersonalization of the human race. Walter Kerr of the *Times* said of the book, "I would call the text childish but children are clearer." Clive Barnes, also in the *Times*, wrote, "I think the basic trouble with the evening is the banality of the book, which has no interest and no point of contact with the audience. It is a difficult show to care for. . . . The story is appallingly weak, and I cannot see why you should have to be bored with it. And the writing is flat and platitudinous. Presumably everyone thought that with a truly sumptuous and adventurous staging, Mr. MacDermot's music would do the trick. This was a miscalculation." The show closed after seven performances, losing even more than *Dude*, $900,000.

Also in 1972, Jim Rado wrote the music and lyrics and, with his brother Ted, the book for a kind of sequel to *Hair*, the rock musical *Rainbow*, which opened off Broadway at the Orpheum Theatre in December. With a hefty score of forty-two songs, it picked up exactly where *Hair* left off, and followed Claude's after-death journey, though it did not explicitly call its central character Claude. Instead the main character was the allegorically named Man, who is killed in Vietnam and finds himself on the "other side," in Rainbow Land. The characters include a mother and father, Jesus Christ, Buddha, a wizard, a girl and her lesbian twin, a stripper, and the President and First Lady. Man goes to Washington to confront the President about Vietnam, and the President sees the horror and absurdity of the war, apologizes to Man, and ends the war. Ironically, in the real world, the

U.S. bombing of Vietnam had stopped and peace talks had begun, but they had fallen apart; on opening night of *Rainbow*, as the show's fictional President agrees to end the war, the real President resumed bombing.

Douglas Watt's review in the *Daily News* was mixed. He wrote, "High spirits and lively music can combine to produce a whale of a party, and, given the advantage of form, they can make for an entertaining evening of theater, too. But although *Rainbow*, which came to the Orpheum last night, is spirited and tuneful, it is also shapeless and, when all is said and done, mere child's play. *Rainbow* is the work of James Rado, coauthor of the book and lyrics for *Hair*. It is a far brighter affair than *Dude*, that recent disaster concocted by Rado's *Hair* collaborators, Gerome Ragni and Galt MacDermot, but it suffers from the same confused notion that *Hair*, which appeared slipshod but possessed a freakish charm, could be reborn."

Clive Barnes of the *Times* liked the show quite a bit. He wrote, "The progenies of *Hair* have not enjoyed a great track record. It is therefore all the more pleasant to report that the latest of that tribe, *Rainbow*, which opened last night at the Orpheum Theater, is a distinct success. It has the style, manner, and energy of *Hair*, as well as its chaotic organization and its simplistic view of a far from simple world. . . . The musical is joyous and life-assertive. It is the first musical to derive from *Hair* that really seems to have the confidence of a new creation about it, largely derived from James Rado's sweet and fresh music and lyrics. . . . It is a brilliant score, full of the most astonishing variety. Some of it does sound like the great Galt MacDermot score for *Hair*, and the influence of MacDermot is strongly felt. But there is also country music, band music, showbiz pastiche, all manner of music, held into one homogenous score by its characteristic forcefulness. . . . What separates *Rainbow* from the other rock and plotless musicals that have recently been going bump in the night is its stylistic cohesion and lack of pretensions. It is not only noisy and brash, it is also very likable."

The most successful of the three all-original post-*Hair* shows, *Rainbow* still ran only forty-eight performances. As this goes to press, Jim Rado is reworking *Rainbow* and still has high hopes for another, more successful production.

Dude, Via Galactica, and *Rainbow* all seem to have suffered from unclear stories and insufficiently integrated scores. Walter Kerr wrote, "Rock musicals, if they are to sustain themselves as genuine theater pieces rather than arena concerts, are going to have to meet the obligations earlier musicals have accepted always with difficulty, often with pain. Music is the ultimate making of any musical. But the music must have something to stand on, something other than its own beat to move it, something to demand one particular song rather than another at a particular moment." But couldn't Kerr have been writing that about *Hair*? Hadn't *Hair* rejected those traditional rules of integrated songs in favor of a more Brechtian, alternative style of theatre? Certainly, with *Hair* a revolution had begun and its revolutionaries were still striving to continue in that fall of 1972, but either they were going in the wrong direction or the commercial theatre just wasn't ready.

The *Hair* of the Nineties

In fact, Kerr also could have been writing about *Rent*. Originally, the idea for *Rent*, the 1996 megahit rock musical, was Billy Aronson's, a young playwright who saw the similarities between *La Bohème's* artists at the turn of the last century in Paris and the young artists at the turn of this century in America. In 1989, he was looking for a composer to collaborate with and Playwrights Horizons suggested Jonathan Larson. When the two met, Aronson said to Larson, "It's time for a new *Hair*." And that is, to some extent, what *Rent* turned out to be, though it's much more conventional in its construction.

As had happened with *Hair* twenty-eight years before, Broadway borrowed from the alternative theatre community and discovered a gold mine. Like *Hair* did, *Rent* brought forbidden content to Broadway and ended up a commercial success. As happened with *Hair*, *Rent* became a cultural phenomenon. The *Rent* cast found themselves in the *New York Times, Newsweek, Vanity Fair, Rolling Stone,* and *Harper's Bazaar.* They appeared on the *Late Show with David Letterman,* the *Charlie Rose Show,* and the *Tonight Show,* and sang "Seasons of Love" at the 1996 Democratic National Convention.

And just as Jim Rado is an Aquarius, Jonathan Larson was likewise born (and died) under the sign of Aquarius, fitting for the man who wanted to write the *Hair* for the nineties. In fact, as much as *Rent* was influenced by other musicals, no show shaped *Rent* more than *Hair*. The two shows are alike in so many ways. Both originated off Broadway and moved to Broadway. Both intentionally cast some actors who had no stage experience at all. Both used costumes that came from thrift stores and actors' closets to add a sense of realism. Neither show had much set. Both shows were a fascinating mix of concert and musical (like the subsequent off Broadway sensation *Hedwig and the Angry Inch*), with both scores relying to some degree on list songs (even sharing some of the same references, to sodomy, marijuana, Ginsberg, Antonioni, and other things). Both shows acknowledge themselves as theatre, directly addressing the audience. Both shows are about drugs (marijuana in *Hair*, heroin in *Rent*), death (Vietnam in *Hair*, AIDS in *Rent*), and a strong sense of family and community. Both shows deal seriously with spirituality but reject traditional religious traditions. Both productions also rejected traditional Broadway staging techniques, and both borrowed techniques from the experimental theatre movement, because both directors came from the experimental theatre community. The static, presentational staging of "Seasons of Love" in *Rent* was considered revolutionary by some but it was in fact taken directly from Tom O'Horgan's staging of "Let the Sun Shine In" in *Hair*. Both shows were perceived to have plot problems (very little conventional plot in *Hair*, a messy plot in *Rent*), and in fact both shows were meant to feel messy and unpolished—to feel as it they were "happening" spontaneously in front of us.

Hair Today

Jim Rado has been working hard on creating a final, "definitive" *Hair* script, one that best defines the intentions of its creators, a version that will bring *Hair* to future generations. This new script contains the song "Sheila Franklin," as well as three new songs, "Hippie Life," "Give Up All Desires," and "The War" (instrumental).

In 2001, New York's *Encores!* Series, concert versions of "lost" or ignored musicals, inexplicably programmed *Hair* into its season, leaving many fans wondering how on earth the score to *Hair* could be considered lost or ignored. The reviews were generally good. Ben Brantley, in the *Times*, wrote, "The dewiness of the cast members as they materialize in phalanxes does indeed give you a wistful rush. But the feeling doesn't really come from nostalgia for a time when promiscuity and drug use seemed penalty-free. No, it's about a less period-specific sense of all that unpolluted potential in one place." But there were dissenters. *Time* magazine said, "It is an artifact of its age, like lava lamps and tie-dyed pants. And, in the *Encores!* revival, it begins by sounding creaky. 'Aquarius,' the show's opening anthem—glorious as originally sung by pure-voiced, then-teenage Ronnie Dyson—was entrusted to Eric Millegan, who was frequently flat on opening night. 'Easy to Be Hard' got a studiously overwrought rendition by Idina Menzel; this pensive lament, which explodes into anguish only during the bridge, was debased into the orgasmic wail of a '90s diva." The review goes on to mention audience members walking out at intermission.

A few months later, the similar *Reprise!* series in Los Angeles staged its own concert version. *Daily Variety* said, "This production . . . doesn't do much more than take a cultural artifact, scrub it until it's inauthentically shiny, and give it a technological audio polish. Make no mistake about it: this show is unrelentingly entertaining, but this is *Hair* as predigested commercial behemoth, not *Hair* as the happening it's supposed to be." The review goes on, "A director has a challenge with *Hair* to make it into more than just a standard period piece. But in this case, Arthur Allan Seidelman doesn't even try to do more; he's just the master logistician rather than an imaginative force. When actors wade out into the audience to dance with the members of the crowd, it's all very cutesy, which is a quality this show emits constantly. It's even a bit condescending to its material."

Michael Butler had planned for a cross-country "festival tour" of *Hair*. His idea was to create a traveling compound, a kind of movie backlot, modeled on two of the most celebrated American hippie hangouts: the Haight-Ashbury neighborhood of San Francisco and Greenwich Village in New York. He wrote, "[The tour's] spiritual design is to present entertainment to the public in an exciting and meaningful way. The sixties were the last great moment in time where we took a hard look at ourselves and asked why. *Hair*, one of the most successful musicals of our time, is considered to be the single entertainment event that represented the very heart and soul of the era. With that in mind, the creators of the *Hair* festival tour believe that the emotion and vision of the sixties will be quite useful to us as a society as we consider the new Millennium. As Aquarius continues to rise and the information age dawns, the *Hair* festival tour is designed to remind us of where we were, where we are, and where we are going." As this book goes to press, plans for the festival tour have been shelved, but a national tour of some less ambitious sort is still being planned.

◤ It's a Dirty Little War

The Tribe

Every cast of *Hair* is called "The Tribe," and in each production of *Hair* around the world, the cast chooses a tribe name. They generally name themselves after a Native American tribe. The practice is not just cosmetic. This show, perhaps more than any other, is an ensemble piece, one in which the entire cast must work together, must like each other, and must often work as a single organism. All the sense of family, of belonging, of responsibility and loyalty inherent in the word "tribe," has to be felt by the cast. Choosing a tribe name begins that process in a very visceral way.

As in Stephen Sondheim and George Furth's musical *Company*, the characters in *Hair* are greatly—and intentionally—underwritten. Much of what is important about the characters is in the subtext, hidden below what feels like very casual, even trivial conversation. It's the job of the actor and director to read between the lines, to discover the relationships, the loyalties, the tensions, the love, and the deep connections among the characters.

George Berger and Claude Bukowski (Jim Rado's mother's maiden name, but coincidentally also the surname of Beat generation poet Charles Bukowski) are the center of the tribe and of the show. Berger, the "psychedelic teddy bear" (a term pinched from the *New York Times* review of the first production), is a manic master of ceremonies. He leads the tribe (and the audience) through the craziness of Act I, late in the act fading into the background to some extent as Claude's story takes center stage. Act I is Berger's act as he introduces the tribe, their philosophy, and their way of life; Act II belongs to Claude, his drug trip, and his decision to go to war, where he will die.

Berger and Claude are two halves of one whole. Claude is the intellectual half, the introspective one, the voice of reason, morality, spirituality, guilt. He's the one who tries to *understand* everything around him, including that which is not understandable—and that's his downfall. He says several times that he is "Aquarius, destined for greatness or madness," but in actuality, he is destined for both. His greatness is in forcing the tribe (through his death) to confront the evils of the world; his madness is his decision to become part of the machinery of war. If Claude is Aquarius, then the opening number is summoning him. (Notice that the tribe's final goodbyes to Claude also take place while singing "Aquarius.") Berger, on the other hand, is the animal half, focused on instinct, courage, pleasure, primal urges. But those primal urges are not just for food, water, and sex— they are also to protect the tribe, to be its leader. Only together do Berger (the id) and Claude (the superego) make one healthy person. (This is a common device in literature, most recently used in the novel and film *The Fight Club*, and also used in the late 1960s in "The Enemy Within," an episode of the original *Star Trek* series.)

With this in mind, it's interesting that both Berger and Claude want Sheila, since they are two halves of a whole. Berger wants Sheila only for the physical pleasures of sex; Claude wants her for the spiritual pleasures of pure love. Only together do they make the perfect lover. Sheila loves Berger, but Berger's only interest in her is physical. When she brings him the gift of a shirt in Act I, his reaction speaks volumes. He feels smothered by her. He doesn't want gifts. He doesn't want commitment, and he doesn't want the depth of feeling he sees in Sheila. As men have done for centuries, his reaction to the smothering love she gives him is to become a jerk, to treat her badly in order to get her to leave him alone. He explodes at her over nothing, hoping she'll hate him, hoping she'll crawl away, licking her wounds, giving him at least temporary freedom. She tries to hang on, tries to laugh off his insults, but eventually she lashes back with the song "Easy to Be Hard." She doesn't understand him. Each time they have sex, each kind word he says to her gives her hope that he really does love her, but he doesn't understand that he's sending these signals. To him, it's just sex. To her, it's love. In the earlier, off Broadway script, Berger cares so little for Sheila (or at least so much more for Claude), that in Act II he even asks Sheila to sleep with Claude before he goes off to war.

One of Berger's big songs, "Going Down," is often overlooked, but its lyric is funny, interesting, and illuminating. The title has two meanings. The first and most literal meaning describes Berger's descent into hell for his sins. He compares (sarcastically) his expulsion from high school to Lucifer's expulsion from heaven, questioning the accepted notion that mainstream education is necessarily the Great Good that everyone thinks it is. But the title also conjures the image of oral sex, maybe the most appropriate meaning for Berger, dismissing another accepted notion that sexuality is forbidden and sinful. But Berger also compares his expulsion to the freeing of the slaves, invoking the Emancipation Proclamation, Abraham Lincoln (who'll show up again later in the show), and the Fourth of July (Independence Day). It's interesting that the principal refers to the ubiquitous generation gap as World War III, a chilling trivialization of the then current Vietnam War. As the song ends, Berger implies that going down to hell may be the better choice after all. After the song ends, the next voice that is heard is Claude, entering and calling himself the Son of God. That's no accident. He is there to lift Berger back up.

Claude Hooper Bukowski, Superstar

It's fascinating how much Claude is compared to Christ in *Hair*. Several times throughout the show, Claude talks about wanting to be invisible, wanting to know what people are thinking, and wanting to perform miracles. Midway through Act I, Claude enters saying, "I am the Son of God. I shall vanish and be forgotten." Is he saying that organized religion has lost touch with God and forgotten the true meaning of Jesus' teachings? Following this comment, Claude comes through the audience and the tribe "blessing" people as he goes. Later, he compares his hair to that of Jesus in the song "Hair." At one point, Jeanie says that "Claude is hung up on a cross over Sheila and

Berger." After the drug trip he says he wants to hang on a cross and eat cornflakes. At the end of the show, when Claude returns to the tribe for the finale, he says, "Berger, I feel like I died." Like Christ, Claude has died and has returned, and like Christ, Claude is the Chosen One, the one member of the tribe chosen (literally, by the draft board) to give his life for the others. In the last moment of the show, Berger forms a cross over Claude as the final lights fade.

In addition to these very obvious moments, there are other less direct references. Like Christ, Claude is sent to his death by the government. Like Christ, Claude suffers enormous confusion and conflict over what to do—Claude throughout Act I and specifically in "Where Do I Go?," Christ in the Garden of Gethsemane. Just as Claude's parents disapprove of him and his lifestyle, there is evidence in the Bible that Jesus' mother and brothers thought he was out of his mind and an embarrassment to the family. And just as the second half of the Bible (the New Testament) focuses on Jesus Christ, the second half of *Hair* shifts its focus almost exclusively to Claude and the story of his death and (metaphorical) resurrection.

It's important to remember that Jesus was not just the Son of God—he was a radical political activist in the same spirit as the political activists of the 1960s. He was the center of a great revisionist social movement that rejected the social and spiritual status quo, dozens of small messianic groups each thinking their leader was the messiah the Jews had been waiting for. As he preached, Jesus roamed the country, living a life of relative poverty, taking handouts of food and shelter from strangers, picking up supporters and adherents as he went, speaking on social and spiritual issues, challenging the authority of the government and the ruling classes, declaring that things must change. When the crowds grew too big to fit inside churches, Jesus began speaking outside in large open areas, and thousands would gather to listen to him and to commune with each other and nature, not unlike the be-ins of the sixties. The hippies' drug trip the night before Claude goes off to his death in war could even be compared to the Last Supper.

Furthermore, if Claude is Jesus, then Berger is John the Baptist, and Jeanie is Mary Magdalene. Even Claude's and Berger's names, by accident or not, are similar to their Biblical counterparts—Claude and Christ, George Berger and John the Baptist. Berger's first speech to the audience deals a lot with water, creating an arguable connection to John the Baptist. At one point, one of the tribe actually cites

John the Baptist as his hero. In fact, the historical John the Baptist was a lot like Berger, wild, out of the mainstream, roaming the countryside, a strong and harsh critic of the government and of the church. Like the hippies of the 1960s, John the Baptist believed the church had lost touch with God, that he and his followers had to discard accepted mainstream religion totally in order to find God. John the Baptist wore camel skins and ate bugs and wild honey. He had wild, long hair and a long, unkempt beard. He was a first-century hippie, vigorously rejecting the establishment and the moral and political status quo. Just as Claude is drawn to Berger, so Jesus was drawn to the radical revolutionary John the Baptist, a charismatic young man declaring philosophical war on the church, the government, and other adult institutions. And like the hippies, most of the followers of John the Baptist were very young.

Because Claude is the emotional and moral center of *Hair*, Jeanie is by virture of her love for him the most important female character in the show, even though it might not appear that way at first glance. She acts as Greek chorus several times throughout the show, explaining things to the audience, identifying characters and relationships, but she also gets a solo introduction song in Act I ("Air") along with the other leads. It's through her that we feel the tragedy and the anguish of those Claude will leave behind. There are cryptic references throughout the show that Jeanie may be psychic in some way (or at least some kind of hippie mystic), that she knows Claude will end up going to war, and that she may know that Claude will die in Vietnam.

It may even be that Jeanie is denying the fact that Claude is the father of her unborn child only to free him from any responsibility, since she knows he doesn't really love her. It's probable that they have slept together. Though there's nothing in the text that says this explicitly, Jeanie and Claude allude to it in their conversation before the be-in, and it's certainly an interesting idea for actors to explore. Though Claude is in love with Sheila, Jeanie is in love with Claude and, along with Berger, she will suffer the greatest loss when Claude dies.

It's hard not to see parallels to Mary Magdalene. As in the Mary Magdalene–Jesus relationship, Jeanie loves Claude, but he can't return her love. (According to "new" lost gospels discovered in 1945, these parallels may even be romantic. Although these new papyrus texts have holes and gaps, some scholars maintain that they describe a romantic relationship between Jesus and Mary Magdalene. Unsurprisingly, this is hotly contested among Biblical scholars.) In any case, like Mary Magdalene, who was called both prostitute and saint, Jeanie provides a symbolic bridge between sexuality and spirituality, between the pleasures of the flesh and the cultivation of the soul. (Perhaps she should be the one to sing "Sodomy.") Jeanie is promiscuous, already pregnant when the show begins (purportedly by "some speed freak"), but she is also the one who invites the audience to the be-in, an event of spiritual exploration and awakening. She brings Claude a book on astral projection, and as mentioned earlier, she seems to have mystical powers.

All that aside, Mary Magdalene would have been right at home with Berger and the tribe. Mary grew up in Magdala, a small fishing village that was a hotbed of rebel activity against the Roman Empire. She came from a well-to-do family, just as many of the sixties hippies came from upper-middle-class families. And, in fact, Mary Magdalene was not a prostitute even though she was characterized as such for centuries, just as the hippies were often characterized as sexual deviants and hedonists. Some texts suggest that she did have a considerable sexual appetite, and because she was well off enough that she didn't have to work, she may have practiced what the hippies of the 1960s called "free love." For that she was considered a sinner by her contemporaries.

Mary Magdalene was an independent thinker who met Jesus, a radical political activist, and joined his movement, a movement dedicated to finding enlightenment, rejecting old social norms and rules, and discovering the answers to the great existential questions; the parallels to the hippie tribe in *Hair* are obvious. After Christ's crucifixion, and after Mary's subsequent preaching and evangelism, she retired to a secluded wilderness where she lived out her remaining years. Some accounts say that each day she was carried up to the heavens by angels to listen to the music of the heavens, an experience probably akin to astral projection, a practice Jeanie is very interested in.

What a Piece of Work Is Claude

Despite the many Christ references, it's also easy to see Claude as a metaphoric Hamlet, the melancholy hippie, prisoner of indecision.

In fact, there are several Shakespeare references in the show. In the original off Broadway script, Claude recites a speech from *Hamlet* to Berger after the drug trip, a speech in which Claude/Hamlet marvels at the nobility and great potential of mankind but confesses that he sees the world as nothing but a barren wasteland. Galt MacDermot later set this speech to music for Broadway, called it "What a Piece of Work Is Man," and it became part of Claude's trip, still serving basically the same purpose, but now sung by two other members of the tribe as part of Claude's hallucination (so arguably still coming from Claude). In the latest version of the script, some of the song's lines have been given back to Claude.

After the trip, as Berger and Claude are waking up, Berger says, "Face reality, Shakespeare." Is that just a coincidence, or does Berger know Claude's trip included a speech from *Hamlet*? Does Berger possess some kind of Shakespearean magical powers that allow him to see inside Claude's mind? Or had Berger been manipulating Claude's trip like a latter day Prospero to persuade him to decide not to go to Vietnam? "What a Piece of Work Is Man" also proves how literate Claude is—if *Hamlet* shows up in his trip, Claude must be familiar with the play and its themes. And of course, by this logic, Claude has read Allen Ginsberg's poem "Wichita Vortex Sutra," on which the other song in the trip, "Three-Five-Zero-Zero," is based—a further illustration that many of the hippies were well educated and well read. Claude also (perhaps coincidentally) quotes earlier from another of Ginsberg's poems—the line "Down to the river," in the song "Where Do I Go?"

At the end of the show, Claude comes back to the tribe, now invisible as he always wished. He sings a reprise of "Manchester, England" as the tribe sings in counterpoint "Eyes Look Your Last," its text taken from *Romeo and Juliet*. This section ends with Hamlet's last words before he dies, "The rest is silence." (There's also another quote from *Hamlet,* which precedes the song "Mess O' Dirt," cut from the show.)

And just as Hamlet was fascinated with plays and players, Claude is fascinated with film. In his Act I introduction, "Manchester, England," he lists as his heroes the legendary film directors Federico Fellini, Michelangelo Antonioni, and Roman Polanski. In both the off Broadway and early Broadway scripts, a scene is included in which Claude makes Sheila act out a scene from a screenplay Claude has been writing about the tribe, just as Hamlet writes a play about the murder of his father by his uncle. "The Flesh Failures" makes a reference to film as well.

Claude Hooper Bukowski, Beat Poet?

In addition to the clear references to Christ and Hamlet, a veneer of 1960s lore overlays Claude via the name he coincidentally shares with Beat poet Charles Bukowski, a lonely, crazy wanderer–poet whose work had become well known by this time. Charles Bukowski was born in 1920 in Germany and moved with his parents to America when he was three. He was first published in the 1940s but gave up his writing for many years. He roamed from job to job and from bar to bar, and his life seemed frequently to border on insanity and death, a theme that showed up in much of his writing and a theme that shows up in Claude's life as well ("destined for greatness or madness"). Charles Bukowski's poems and novels were filled to overflowing with existential angst, intoxication, suicide attempts, and an unnerving, sometimes deeply disturbing view of life. Claude is surely kin to Charles Bukowski, and his surname provides (even if accidentally) a kind of shorthand description—at least to audiences of the original production—of Claude's worldview and his stumbling journey toward Understanding. Like Claude, Charles Bukowski had an abusive father. Like Claude, Charles Bukowski was an outsider. And as Claude wishes to be "invisible," Charles Bukowski was metaphorically invisible during his teen years, when terribly disfiguring acne made him a complete social outsider, utterly ignored by his peers. Of course, Claude and Charles Bukowski differ in one important way. Charles Bukowski believed there was no meaning in life; he once said, "I am not a man who looks for solutions in God or politics." But Claude is sure there is profound meaning in life, if only he could find it, and he looks both to God and to politics for that meaning.

As an artist, Charles Bukowski could also be seen as a model for Claude's alter ego, Jim Rado, and Rado's partner, Jerry Ragni. Just as Bukowski rejected most of the conventions of American poetry, trying to break through to something new, so Rado and Ragni were trying to do the same with the American musical. Like the creators of *Hair*, Bukowski believed his chosen art form was dying, mired in tired conventions of yesteryear, devoid of innovation or surprise, fat and contented. He wanted to challenge the status quo, to address and portray reality in a raw, brash, antiliterary style, speaking in the voice not of The Writer but of the average American. Bukowski mixed together a remarkable ear for everyday language with a deft use of abstract imagery, just as Ragni and Rado did in *Hair*. Bukowski once said, "Genius is the ability to say a profound thing in a simple way." His description could easily be applied to nearly every scene in *Hair*, particularly to the lyrics of *Hair's* songs. Certainly the last lines of the show, the repeated "Let the sun shine in," became among the most powerful words ever spoken in the theatre, verbalizing a devastating, profound idea in the simplest of terms. Mirroring the birth of *Hair* and its discovery by the mainstream, Bukowski's work was at first known by just a few, finding an outlet only by way of underground presses and magazines, but soon his exciting new style—or perhaps, more accurately, his exciting new *rejection* of style—found an audience and he became an acknowledged Great American Writer. When Charles Bukowski died in 1994, he had written over sixty books. Yet throughout his career many critics dismissed his work as boring and flat; and many contemporary critics still do so, just as many people today refuse to see the depth, the complexity, the genius of *Hair*. True, today not many people may catch the allusion hidden in Claude's surname, but it was unmistakable when *Hair* opened.

Myth Appropriation

Claude and his journey also run parallel to the greatest and most enduring myths. The great human myths try to ask fundamental questions about human existence—why we're here, whether or not there's a God, what our relationship to that God may be, what we'll leave behind, and so much more. The myths tell us who the bad guys are (even when they are us), what will be expected of us, and how we must face the challenges ahead. In asking and sometimes answering those questions, all the great myths from all the great civilizations—Ancient Greece or Rome, Africa, Asia, Europe, America, South America, wherever—share characters, stories, themes, and universal truths, even though their specifics may echo their time and place. The characters may include various versions of heroes, princesses, wizards, and dragons. And just as many of the greatest films of the twentieth century fit into that mythic tradition (*Star Wars*, perhaps, more than any other), so too does *Hair*, although with some fundamental differences.

In Charles Champlin's book *George Lucas: The Creative Impulse*, Champlin examines *Star Wars* as myth, and he writes, "What the myths revealed to Lucas, among other things, was the capacity of the human imagination to conceive alternate realties to cope with reality." Wasn't that exactly what the American hippie culture was doing in the 1960s, exploring alternate realities to try to understand and explain the insanity of the real world? Maybe America in 1967 needed a new myth more than at any other time in its history, and maybe in that turbulent time the only possible new myth had to be different from all that had gone before.

The most common ancient myth is the Hero's Journey, so it is fitting that the symbols and images of the great myths in *Hair* are found primarily in Claude's journey. The journey myth begins with a "call" of some kind, either from within or from an outside source in the form of a message or vision. Initially the hero refuses the call and clings to the known, to the comfortable, to the familiar. But eventually the hero must make the choice to separate himself from his community, from his old world, to go on his required journey to an unknown land. Along the way, he must endure various tests, rituals, and obstacles. One of those tests is the "one forbidden thing," which shows up in hundreds of stories, from Genesis (and most other creation stories) to *Star Wars* to *Willy Wonka and the Chocolate Factory*. He must go through an initiation to *earn* his manhood and then return with his new knowledge and maturity to share with others—in other words, to leave behind his childhood and return as an adult. As myth expert Joseph Campbell once said in an interview with Bill Moyers, "What all the myths have to deal with is transformations of one kind of another. You have been thinking one way, you now have to think a different way." Central figures from every major religion—Moses, Jesus, Muhammad, Buddha, and others— went on similar "vision quests."

Most mythic heroes find along the way a guide or magician or some other mystical creature who helps them begin, who lays out the rules, who imparts important wisdom that will come in handy later. But this guide can only go so far with the hero, and often dies or is imprisoned partway through the adventure. After all, it's the hero's journey. Still, before the guide leaves, he gives the hero a magic weapon or amulet. The hero may pick up other companions along the way, but his ultimate test (for Luke Skywalker, for instance, destroying the Death Star) must be taken alone.

The world into which the hero travels is usually strange and magical and dangerous, a kind of murky version of the hero's own unconscious, full of his deepest fears, his strangest fantasies, his greatest hopes and ambitions; and as in dreams, it's not always clear what's safe and dangerous, what's good and evil. As Sondheim wrote in *Into the Woods*, witches can be right and giants can be good. Often the hero encounters a labyrinth or maze, one of the great symbols of human life, always twisting, turning, full of dead ends, surprise turns, and doubling back. It is the ultimate search for a pattern, for a kind of sense in life. It also may represent a journey through the complexity of the human mind and emotions, in a quest to reach the central, essential truth of "who I am." Sometimes a forest or jungle serves as the maze, particularly in cultures that hold trees as sacred. Sometimes the hero must descend into the underworld.

Ultimately, the hero must make a major sacrifice of some sort and prove himself through a heroic deed before he can return home. The deed can be physical (winning a war, saving a life) or spiritual (discovering a Great Truth or finding Answers). Finally, at the end of the story, the hero returns, utterly transformed, and balance is restored to the universe.

Everyone must go through the hero's transformation, if not physically then spiritually. Everyone must "die" as a child and be "reborn" as an adult. Most of us can't actually go on a heroic quest and commit acts of great bravery, so our journeys happen inside. Claude's journey happens both inside (during the drug trip) and outside (in Vietnam). In *Hair* (mostly in Act II), Claude's two interlocking journeys, one culminating in a spiritual deed and the other culminating in a physical deed, mirror the two realms of exploration the hippie culture was concerned with. They wanted to find God but they also wanted to fix what was wrong with America.

Claude begins by refusing the "call" (his draft notice), electing to evade the draft like all his friends. But we see his ambivalence in his reticence to burn his draft card. In Act II, he goes off alone for three days on a kind of vision quest, and then makes the choice that he will allow himself to be drafted and go to war, to go off into the mystical, dangerous jungle that is Vietnam. He begins the first of his two related journeys with The Trip. Berger acts as Claude's mystical guide and gives Claude a joint laced with mescaline and peyote (his amulet?), and through the labyrinth of surrealism (the unknown land of hallucination), Claude encounters obstacles and dangers galore as he navigates the maze of his own mind. One could even argue Claude is tested with the "one forbidden thing" in the form of illegal drugs. During his trip, he also runs into individuals from the various cultures that have given us our great myths: Africans, Native Americans, Asians, a general and two fictional characters from the "old" American South, Lincoln, a movie actor, a soul singer, and a figure from the 1960s civil rights movement. He finds himself in the dark, scary jungle/forest, along with all his friends, but they all get shot and killed, leaving Claude to finish his first journey on his own.

Having successfully navigated this first set of tests and obstacles, he starts off on the second leg of his journey (going to the real war), and he says goodbye to his "traveling" companions and his mystic guide, Berger. Berger cannot go with him to Vietnam, the second unknown land. Claude goes to war (the underworld?), hoping to make that transformation, hoping to Become a Man. But Claude's story ends prematurely. Unlike all other mythic heroes, Claude dies before he can finish his journey. The "wrongness" of the Vietnam War screws up Claude's myth. He never gets to slay a dragon or find the grail. He makes a sacrifice as all heroes must, but in this case, he sacrifices his own life and it's involuntary, almost accidental. He does not get to come back home to share what he has learned. His world does not come back into balance. Most mythic heroes encounter each test just as they become ready for it, but Claude faces one test he can never be ready for, being dropped in a jungle to be shot at by hidden snipers. *Hair* does not allow balance to be restored.

Or has Claude actually moved on to a higher level of existence? Has he graduated from our world to the next, the way the great mythic heroes had to graduate from adolescence to adulthood, from ignorance to wisdom? Are the Vietcong the monster Claude must slay or is the immorality of war the monster? Or is the inhuman power of the U.S. government (in the form of "the system" or the draft) the monster, just like Darth Vader? Is the mescaline/peyote-laced joint Claude's magic amulet, or is his army-issued rifle? Does Berger, Claude's guide, help him or not? Is the trip supposed to be Claude's only journey, the journey that teaches him and transforms him? Is that what Berger intended? Is Berger Claude's Obi-Wan Kenobi telling Luke Skywalker to "use the force," hoping Claude will discover the truth in himself with a little help from the hallucinogenic smoke? (The experience many people describe when under the influence of hallucinogens is strikingly similar to the way *Star Wars* describes "the force.") Should Claude's journey have ended with the drug trip—rather than in Vietnam—with a new understanding of the nature of existence, like the journeys of Christ and Buddha before him?

Like all heroes, Claude must make a sacrifice for a greater good, but he has what few mythic heroes have: a choice of sacrifice. He can sacrifice his safety to preserve democracy and (allegedly) protect his country against the spread of Communism. Or he can sacrifice his personal freedom to protest an unjust war and (it is hoped) help demonstrate the immorality of the war. He can make his heroic sacrifice no matter which way he comes down on the issue of the Vietnam War. Also, interestingly, Claude does return in a way at the end, but only as a ghost and unable to impart any of his hard-earned knowledge to his friends. *Hair's* myth cannot end traditionally, because the world was upside down in the late 1960s, hopelessly out of balance, and a happy ending would have been dishonest and at odds with the show's central message that the audience is responsible and must take action before it's too late. In a way, *Hair* acts contrary to myth. While a myth seeks to explain the unexplainable and answer universal questions, *Hair* seeks to ask important questions that have not been answered and hopes to move the audience to ask these questions themselves.

One specifically American myth is the western, the cowboy story. But *Hair* sees the lie at the core of the western, just as America itself was becoming disenchanted with westerns during the Vietnam War. *Hair* sees that the frontier cannot always be tamed, that our history as a country won with guns is not necessarily honorable, that killing is not heroic or good nor is it usually the best way to resolve a problem. Throughout the 1940s and 1950s, the western was a fantasy world in which Americans could work out issues about sex, race, gender, and violence. But that was a time when America still saw itself as the ultimate Good Guy. The Vietnam War robbed us of that. Our self-image was tarnished, and much of America now began seeing itself as a bully. The myth of the western no longer worked, and it would be transformed over the years in films like *Westworld*, *Silverado*, *Unforgiven*, and others. It's interesting that in the film version of *Hair*, Claude is portrayed as something of a cowboy.

Hippie Get Your Gun

So why *does* Claude choose to go to war? After so much pressure from the tribe to burn his draft card, after his terrifying hallucinations about agonizing death during his drug trip, why does he go to Vietnam? In a literary sense, he is destined to go. He's the Chosen One, the one who will sacrifice himself for the others. But on a personal level, Ragni and Rado have painted a portrait of a very real, very complex person. From the very beginning of the show, we find out that Claude is searching for fulfillment, trying to find himself and his place in the world. In fact, that is why he has joined the hippies. In his first song, "Manchester, England," Claude says that he "dropped out," as hippie and drug guru Timothy Leary advocated, but that his life is still unfulfilling. He asks Timothy Leary directly in the song why this is, why his life should still feel so meaningless when he has followed Leary's instructions. Like the title character in *Pippin*, Claude is on a quest to find the meaning of life, and his song "Where Do I Go?" is all about his search for answers, for spiritual awakening, for God. He has looked everywhere they've told him to look, but the answers to life still evade him. Where does he go now? Like young men throughout history, Claude decides that war may just be the thing that makes a man of him, that shows him who he really is. Although for Pippin war is just a comic sketch performed by a troupe of players, for Claude war is very real. He may find out who he is, but he may also get killed. After the drug trip, Claude realizes that although war scares him, nothing else in life has proved satisfying.

But here *Hair* again breaks the rules. Instead of finding his true self deep in the jungles of Vietnam, instead of experiencing revelations about himself, instead of gaining elusive wisdom about the nature of life, Claude is dropped into Vietnam and instantly killed by a North Vietnamese sniper. There is no romance here, no epiphanies, no triumph for our hero. He just gets shot and dies in the jungle, running away, screaming like a frightened child. It reminds us that war is not a John Wayne movie or a romance novel. War is death.

Three-Five-Zero-Zero

Once the U.S. Congress had given President Lyndon Johnson the power to do pretty much anything he wanted in Vietnam, he decided to send in ground troops to secure air bases and begin a full-scale ground war, marking the official escalation of the war. On the morning of March 8, 1965, three thousand, five hundred Marines—the first ground troops of the war—came ashore near the Da Nang airbase, welcomed by Vietnamese girls and four American advisers holding a bedsheet proclaiming "Welcome to the Gallant Marines."

But that may not be what the song "Three-Five-Zero-Zero" in *Hair* refers to. Jim Rado has said that the song was inspired by an Alan Ginsberg poem. Ginsberg's "Wichita Vortex Sutra," written in February, 1966, contains almost all the freaky, violent, surrealistic images in the song "Three-Five-Zero-Zero," often quoted word for word. In the poem, General Maxwell Taylor proudly reports to the press that three thousand, five hundred of the enemy were killed in one month. He repeats the number, digit by digit, for effect: "Three-Five-Zero-Zero." In addition, Ginsberg's reference to 256 Vietcong killed and 31 captured finds its way into the song lyric as 256 Vietcong *captured*. Though the song starts out somber and intense, spilling out Ginsberg's images of death and dying, it turns midway into a manic dance number, an absurdist celebration of killing that echoes Maxwell's glee at reporting the enemy casualties, commenting on the happy face that the U.S. government tried to put on the ever diminishing returns of the war in Vietnam. While our soldiers (and theirs) kept dying, Washington tried to whip up World War II–style support for the war among Americans. But we had seen the war on our TV screens this time, and we weren't celebrating.

Walking in Space

References to the war are peppered throughout the *Hair* script, some of them very subtle, like Sheila's passing mention of the 1967 march on the Pentagon. The only dramatic through-line in the show focuses on Claude's existential angst over the purpose of his life and his dilemma over whether to go to war or burn his draft card. In and beyond the conversations about Claude going to the induction center to be drafted, the war is an ever present image in the show. During Claude's Act II drug trip, the images of war pile up in both comic images and disturbingly dramatic ones. In most productions of *Hair*, it's made clear that Berger gives Claude a "special" joint, one presumably laced with more powerful hallucinogens than the others. Since the hippies believed that some drugs (LSD, peyote, pot, and others) opened and expanded the mind, increasing the power of the mind, helping the user reach higher consciousness and greater understanding, we can assume that Berger gives Claude a more powerful drug specifically to help him clear away his indecision about Vietnam.

The trip begins with the song "Walking in Space," most of which describes the sensations of being high, but there are already a few references to the war here. Once the song is ended, everything else in the trip is triggered by Claude's fear of going to war. The first images are of young men, Claude among them, jumping out of a helicopter into the jungles of Vietnam. When Claude lands, he sees two American soldiers chasing a Vietnamese peasant. He turns around and sees George Washington and his troops, retreating from an attack by Indians. The next image is Ulysses S. Grant assembling his troops, which include Abraham Lincoln, John Wilkes Booth, Calvin Coolidge, Rhett Butler, Scarlett O'Hara, and General Custer, all symbols of war in Claude's mixed-up, drugged mind. Also among Grant's troops is Aretha Franklin, a wonderful non sequitur that might represent Claude's knowledge that the draft is racist—or it might just be the kind of random image a drugged mind conjures. Then again, maybe it's significant that Aretha sings "Indian Love Call," an old-fashioned love song from the 1924 operetta *Rose Marie*, which was made popular by Jeanette MacDonald and Nelson Eddy. Maybe this crazy vision of Aretha Franklin funkifying this operetta song is Claude's image of a new, more racially open definition of love and coupling. Grant's troops dance a minuet for a bit and then are attacked by African witch doctors (probably a reference to Hud, who is referred to as the bogeyman in Act I), and the witch doctors kill everyone but Lincoln. Hud becomes LeRoi Jones, the black social activist, writer, and publisher, and he confronts Lincoln (played by a black woman, by the way), threatening to harpoon him/her, a reference to the black separatists of the sixties, who refused to allow whites to participate in the Civil Rights movement, who refused any help at all from white Americans. (Interestingly, LeRoi Jones didn't like *Hair* and said in one interview, "It has nothing to do with black people.") Lincoln calms Hud/Jones down and proceeds to deliver a crazy, soulful Gettysburg Address.

Many of the historical figures Claude's subconscious conjures up in this trip relate to the way in which he no doubt sees himself and his tribe: George Washington, a man who fought to free his nation from the oppression of injustice, General Grant and President Lincoln, who fought for national unity and the end of racial injustice, and Calvin Coolidge, who fought for international disarmament and who actively supported the Kellogg-Briand Pact of 1928, which renounced war as an instrument of national policy. This roster of historical figures even includes John Wilkes Booth, who (at least in his own mind) rose up against what he saw as a corrupt government in order to preserve his nation and save the lives of men being murdered in what he saw as an unjust war. On the other hand, George Custer also appears in Claude's trip, a man who attacked and murdered hundreds of Indians at Little Big Horn, a moment in history that surely would have appalled Claude's tribe.

As the trip continues, the killing of war comes to the forefront of Claude's mind. A succession of comic stereotypes murder each other—first monks, who are killed by Catholic nuns, who are killed by astronauts, who are killed by Chinese, who are killed by guerillas, who are killed by a Native American. This sequence is played three times, forward and backward, as the trip spins out of control. The action continues as Claude's parents appear with a drill sergeant and have a conversation with a suit Claude has left behind, the only thing that remains after Claude is killed in war. The tribe begins playing children's games that escalate until they all end up murdering one another. The song "Three-Five-Zero-Zero" begins, and the tribe becomes the walking dead, advancing on the audience, accusing them of complicity in the horror of war. By the end of the song, everyone has died again, agonizing, slow deaths. Two tribe members have been watching all this from a platform above the fray and they sing "What a Piece of Work Is Man," an ironic tribute to the majesty, nobility, and *potential*, even if unrealized, of mankind, sung as the two singers descend and walk though the battlefield of slaughtered bodies.

The trip ends with a reprise of a short section of "Walking in Space," and its lyric takes on a whole new meaning here, because this time the words are being sung by a stage full of dead bodies, young people killed in the jungles of Vietnam (a drug-induced version of Vietnam in Claude's mind). Now they are "walking in space" because they are dead; they are ghosts or angels or spirits. Their eyes are "wide open" because they are dead and cannot close them. And in the hereafter, they can see more clearly. Like Emily in *Our Town*, once they die, they can see what life really means:

Walking in space
We find the purpose of peace,
The beauty of life
You can no longer hide.
Our eyes are open
Wide, wide, wide.

And as they have, Claude will soon "walk in space" and finally find his answers as well. *Hair* is all about Claude's journey to find the answers to his existence, and the show can only end once Claude has found them, once his eyes are open and he can find the purpose of peace and see the beauty of life.

Now and Then

After the trip in Act II, the tribe say their goodbyes to Claude in "The Bed" and "Good Morning Starshine." Claude has made his decision, though it is still unspoken. He has decided to let himself be drafted. And the lyric to "Starshine" tells us what's coming—Claude's death in Vietnam:

Good morning starshine,
The earth says hello.
You twinkle above us,
We twinkle below.

The earth will indeed say hello, to Claude's dead body when it is sent home for burial, and Claude will thereafter be only a memory, perhaps looking down from heaven (twinkling above) onto his beloved tribe, as they look up into the heavens for answers (twinkling below). (In fact, a star in the constellation Aquarius has been named for *Hair*.)

In the final scene, the creators of *Hair* play around with time, creating a kind of temporal split-screen effect. Just as time meant nothing during Claude's drug trip, here too it is not linear, perhaps because Claude's real trip—his journey—is not over. After the tribe says goodbye and leaves Claude, we instantly jump ahead a month or more in time and Claude finds himself in the jungles of Vietnam. In the original version (the newest version is slightly different),

Claude sings a fragmented reprise of "Ain't Got No," with the audience's imagination left to fill in the things he "ain't got" now that he's in the jungles of Vietnam. A Vietcong sniper appears and begins shooting at him. Surprisingly, Claude doesn't run and he doesn't shoot back. He just stands and takes it. The fight has gone out of him. In the newest version, he even lays his gun down and surrenders. The sniper chases him into the jungle, and we jump back in time to the morning after the trip, when the tribe marches in protest on the army induction center—a last-minute effort to save Claude and the other young men being sent to their death. As they march, they wait for Claude. They think he is going to join them, but he's nowhere to be found. In fact, he's dead. He's been killed by the Vietcong sniper several months in the future. Present and future have collided in Claude; once he decides to allow himself to be drafted, he is instantly as good as dead. His future is decided. So even though his real death won't be for several months, here on the morning after the trip, he is already dead.

Finally, Claude comes back to the tribe, existing in both times at once, in that temporal split screen, existing both that morning several months into the future on which he is killed, and this morning after the drug trip, to take one last look at his tribe. Now that he is dead, time means nothing. Just as we see through Claude's eyes during the drug trip, the same is true now. We are with Claude "on the other side" and time is fluid.

Eyes Look Your Last

The finale, "The Flesh Failures," summarizes the themes of the show, particularly the insanity of war and our consumerist culture, obsessed with comfort as people were being murdered in Southeast Asia. We pass each other on the street, bundled up in our designer clothes, created and purchased specifically to display our level of wealth and success, too busy to stop and connect with each other, too busy to help the homeless lying on the street, too preoccupied with our superficial lives, our appointments, our scramble to accumulate possessions (a theme *Hair's* descendant *Rent* would return to). The song tells us that somewhere inside, buried beneath all this, hidden deep down, there is greatness in the human race, that we have such potential, but that we have failed. We have failed by succumbing to comfort, to the demands of the flesh, instead of aiming for something higher. Claude comes forward, now dead, killed in Vietnam, invisible to the tribe—just as returning Vietnam vets were often "invisible" in American culture—and as he reprises his theme song, "Manchester, England," the tribe sings in counterpoint "Eyes Look Your Last," a musical setting of a speech from *Romeo and Juliet*. The words are Romeo's, after he finds Juliet's (apparently) dead body and just before he takes his own life. Just as Romeo is looking at the dead body of his beloved Juliet, here the tribe is seeing the death of their beloved Claude. The death is just as senseless, just as unnecessary. The last line of this section, "the rest is silence," is Hamlet's last line before dying at the end of *Hamlet*. Claude, the Hamlet figure, has died, and we are killing ourselves as well, the tribe is telling us. After another verse of "The Flesh Failures," the show finishes with "Let the Sun Shine In."

But "Let the Sun Shine In" is not the happy song some people think it is. It's a call to action. The tribe is begging us, the audience, to change things, to stop the killing, the hatred, the discrimination, the destruction of our world. They are saying that we are in a time of darkness (as described in detail in "The Flesh Failures," "Easy to Be Hard," and other songs), that it is now time to let the sun shine in and change things. It's significant that the lyric doesn't say that the sun is already shining and everything is going to be fine. It says we have to take action, we have to *let* the sun shine on the darkness around us, and the implication is unmistakable—if we don't let the sun shine, it will be the end of us.

6   For God, for Country

In the Name of the Father

LeRoi Jones, black social activist and writer, wrote in the 1960s, "God has been replaced, as he has all over the West, with respectability and air conditioning." And *Hair* reflects that view of American society in the 1960s. It exposes the dark underbelly of organized religion as it satirizes its hypocrisies. In the song "Donna," it's unclear whether Berger is singing about looking for a girl named Donna or, in fact, looking for the Virgin Mary, the *Ma*donna. The song starts with a slight variation of "once upon a time" and the last line of the song actually replaces the words "my Donna" with "Madonna." Could Berger be talking about *the* Madonna, the "sixteen-year-old" Virgin Mary? Could this song be about his search for true spirituality as symbolized by Mary, his inability to find that spirituality in the hypocrisy and institutionalization of organized religion? And could that "disfigured" spirituality be represented by the tattooed Donna? After all, the song catalogs all his attempts to find spirituality, in India, in South America, and (through psychedelic drugs) in San Francisco. In the second part of the song when he calls Donna psychedelic, perhaps he's telling us he found the Virgin Mary—and God—through psychedelic, mind-expanding drugs (which was the goal of the drug users, after all) and that it was only through the drugs that he could "evolve" into a more spiritual being.

Just a few minutes after "Donna," the tribe performs the song "Sodomy," a mock religious hymn cataloguing sexual acts that organized religion condemns: fellatio, cunnilingus, pederasty, and masturbation. It satirizes religion's preoccupation with sex, "unspeakable" acts that nonetheless fill the Bible (making it as R-rated as *Hair*), acts that continue to embarrass the modern-day Catholic church. The audience flinches when pederasty is mentioned, but do we too easily forget that the sexual repression of the Catholic church drives too many priests still today to molest altar boys over and over? Before the song, Woof poses as a priest and says, "This is the body and blood of Jesus Christ. And I am going to eat you. I swear to tell the truth, the whole truth, and nothing but the truth, so help me God. In the name of the Father, the Son, and the Holy Ghost. Amen." In one short speech, he pokes fun at the solemnity of priests and religious rituals, the cannibalistic implications of communion, and the all too blatant exceptions to the Constitutional separation of church and state in America. He then sings "Sodomy," skewering the sexual hypocrisy of organized religion and concluding with a reference to the *Kama Sutra*. This scene also recognizes the parallel between modern religious ritual and theatre, both attempts by humans to make some kind of order out of the chaos of our lives, both with very ancient roots, both performances for an audience. But does this comparison make the religious ritual less legitimate or does it make the theatre performance more legitimate?

The song "Ain't Got No" also makes two religious references. The song is a list of things the hippies "ain't got," with responses shouted out by the tribe. When the soloist sings that he has no faith, the tribe shouts out, "Catholic," suggesting that the Catholics have lost their faith, have lost touch with God in the morass of man-made ritual that defines the church (already satirized in "Sodomy"). At the end of the song, when the soloist sings that he has no God, the tribe shouts, "Good." But we learn throughout the show that the tribe is in fact very spiritual, so this reference means only that it's a good thing to lose God *as defined by modern religions*, a false God, a God loaded up with man's baggage and his desire for control over his fellow humans, a God distanced from real spirituality and faith. *Hair* repeatedly points out the hypocrisy of modern organized religion, including in one of the most potent sections of the song "Hair"—"My hair like

Jesus wore it, hallelujah, I adore it. Hallelujah, Mary loved her son—why don't my mother love me?"

Hair does not disrespect religion or Christianity so much as it ridicules the misuses and exploitation of Christianity. Many so-called Christians used the Bible then and still use it now to control, to bludgeon, to seek power, to tell others how to live their lives, and this is what *Hair* reviles. Still today, many people calling themselves Christians try to legislate morality by claiming that America was founded on "Christian principles" and that our founding fathers were Christians, when the exact opposite is true.

In 1756, in a letter to Charles Cushing, John Adams wrote, "This would be the best of all possible worlds, if there were no religion in it!" In 1816, in a letter to John Quincy Adams, he wrote, "Let the human mind loose. It must be loose. It will be loose. Superstition and dogmatism cannot confine it." In 1823, Thomas Jefferson wrote in a letter to John Adams, "The day will come when the mystical generation of Jesus, by the Supreme Being as his father, in the womb of a virgin, will be classed with the fable of the generation of Minerva in the brain of Jupiter. But we may hope that the dawn of reason and freedom of thought in these United States will do away [with] all this artificial scaffolding." In 1787, in a letter to Peter Carr, Jefferson wrote, "Question with boldness even the existence of God; because if there be one, He must approve the homage of Reason rather than that of blindfolded Fear." In 1820, in a letter to William Short, Jefferson wrote, "I have examined all the known superstitions of the world, and I do not find in our particular superstition of Christianity one redeeming feature. They are all alike founded on fables and mythology." In his famous pamphlet, *The Age of Reason*, Thomas Paine wrote, "All natural institutions of churches, whether Jewish, Christian, or Turkish, appear to me no other than human inventions, set up to terrify and enslave mankind, and monopolize power and profit." Later in the same pamphlet, he wrote, "The most detestable wickedness, the most horrid cruelties, and the greatest miseries that have afflicted the human race have had their origin in this thing called revelation, or revealed religion." In the same document, he wrote, "What is it the Bible teaches us?—rapine, cruelty, and murder." Benjamin Franklin wrote, in his 1758 book *Poor Richard's Almanac*, "Lighthouses are more helpful than churches." It's significant that the U.S. Constitution is the first significant governing charter in the history of mankind that does not invoke any kind of God.

Like the real hippies of the 1960s, *Hair* doesn't limit itself to Christian spirituality. The mantra chanted before the song "Don't Put It Down" ("om mane padme hum") is a scared Buddhist mantra to Avalokiteswara, the Buddhist Savior and Protector. Chanting this mantra invokes the benevolent attention and blessings of Chenrezig, the embodiment of compassion. All the teachings of the Buddha are said to be contained in this one untranslatable mantra, leading toward an understanding of how to remove suffering from all living beings. (Interestingly, Padmé is also a heroic character in the *Star Wars* film series.) Each of the six syllables of the chant helps perfect an aspect of the meditator's nature—ethics, tolerance, patience, perseverance, concentration, and wisdom. Perhaps this chant is placed before the song "Don't Put It Down" as a prayer for the people who have narrow, shallow, intolerant visions of what America is about and what patriotism means, to help open the minds of Americans to what really matters.

As more evidence of the spiritual side of the hippie culture and of *Hair* (and despite, or perhaps because of, the show's criticism of organized religion), the original Broadway cast celebrated its third anniversary in May 1971 by holding a very special mass at the Cathedral of St. John the Divine, in New York City, presided over by Gerry Ragni's brother Richard and other clergy. For the occasion, Galt MacDermot wrote a new Mass in F, and instead of sacred hymns, he used songs from *Hair*, sung by the Broadway cast and several New York choirs. The mass was released on an album called *Divine Hair/Mass in F*.

The Blue, White, and Red

So many people accused the hippies of being "un-American," of disrespecting their country, of ridiculing patriotism. But in fact the hippies were following in the footsteps of great American rebels like John Adams, Sam Adams, Martin Luther King Jr., and others—refusing to let America be less than it could be, demanding that it live up to its potential, that it shine like a beacon to the world as our founding fathers intended. And *Hair* reflects that more genuine—and more controversial—kind of tough-love patriotism.

There are references to patriotism and to the flag throughout the show, sometimes in genuine expressions of love for our country, sometimes in satiric jabs at those who would wrap their bigotry and bloodlust in the flag. Berger is the first to make one, to the Statue of Liberty, in his first monologue leading into "Donna." Sheila quotes "My Country 'Tis of Thee" in "I Believe in Love," making the point that the truly patriotic thing for Americans to do, in the 1960s and still today, is to reject all the hatred and bigotry in our country. In paraphrasing the famous quote, she sings:

> I believe that now is the time
> For all good men to
> Believe in love.
> I believe that now is the time
> For all good men to
> Come to the aid of
> My country 'tis of thee,
> Sweet land of liberty.

Racial discord and discrimination was tearing America in two during this time, and the hippies' message of love and acceptance could have gone a long way in healing America's wounds if the "establishment" had just taken them seriously.

In the song "Hair," the hippies quote "The Star Spangled Banner"—

> Oh say, can you see
> My eyes?
> If you can,
> Then my hair's too short.

The hippies called their long hair their "freak flag," their symbol of freedom and nonconformity. To them, their hair was as potent, as sacred a symbol as the American flag.

"Don't Put It Down" works two ways. First, the song is about loving and respecting America and the idea that political dissent is not un-American, that it is, in fact, uniquely and profoundly American, that it is what our forefathers fought and died for. The singers tell us that though their expression of love for America may be different, though it may be labeled "subversive" by some, though their appearance is unconventional, though they protest and picket, their love for their country is no less sincere, no less profound. Like

Jimi Hendrix's shattering rendition of "The Star Spangled Banner" at Woodstock, "Don't Put It Down" makes the emphatic point that there is more than one way to be patriotic. In the original staging of this song, two of the singers folded the American flag in proper military fashion as they sang, demonstrating that they do respect this symbol of America. (Astronaut Jim Lovell made headlines when he and his wife stormed out of a performance of the Broadway production over what he shallowly perceived as disrespect of the American flag in "Don't Put It Down.")

The other side of this song takes the title literally, laughing at the idea that the flag can never touch the ground. Taken this way, the song suggests humorously that perhaps the self-identified "patriots" who wanted flag burners arrested, who wanted hippie protesters imprisoned, had taken their patriotism too far, that the symbol of America had become more important to them than the country itself, more important than being true to our nation's ideals, that in fact the fervor of these "patriots" had crossed the line into craziness ("crazy for the blue, white, and red"). The constant rearranging of the flag's colors in the lyric suggests that not everyone's love for the United States should have to be expressed the same way. This is where these two different takes on this song come together in a unified message.

Perhaps the last song, "The Flesh Failures," illustrates the hippies' patriotism better than any other moment in the show, because it dramatizes their willingness to *do something* to save their country, to heal it, to solve its problems. They don't just sit back in their cars with an "America—Love It or Leave It" bumper sticker on the back. They don't just make money and watch television, refusing to get involved, refusing to honor Lincoln's "government of the people, by the people, and for the people." They're out there trying to change what's wrong. They're out there *participating* in democracy. They see a "dying nation" that needs saving. They see what America can be—

> *Somewhere, inside something, there is a rush of greatness.*
> *Who knows what stands in front of our lives?*

All There in Black and White

Hair challenges nearly everything we complacently accept as ordinary in life, all the things we just don't think about. It shoves them in our face and demands that we look at them. Racism, obscenity, sexual repression, and other issues are all laid bare before us, rejecting the restrictions of "polite society." In a 1970 interview with *Ebony* magazine, Jim McCloden, who played Hud in Chicago, said, "I get a chance to express anger at white exploitation, slavery, white capitalism, the draft. A chance to be satirical about things black people have known for a long time."

Racism is the most American of all issues. It was an issue when the Declaration of Independence was written. It split the nation during the Civil War and again in the 1960s. In the song "Colored Spade" Hud lists every offensive, racist label and epithet ever thrown at him, to show how horrible, how ridiculous, how offensive they are. He confronts the audience with words and phrases and stereotypes they may have used (or allowed others to use), and he claims them for his own. When we hear them all together, when we realize how many more labels there are for blacks than for whites, they become ridiculous. They lose their power.

In "Dead End," the black tribe members list signs we encounter every day—"Dead End," "Keep Out," "Don't Walk," "No Standing," "Keep Off the Grass," and others. And the fact that these warnings are being sung by black men and women raises them to the level of social metaphor. This is the world black Americans face every day, in employment, in housing, in pay, in opportunity, not just in 1968 but still today.

At the beginning of Act II, two songs, "Black Boys" and "White Boys," make a powerful statement without the audience's even noticing. It's surprising enough (especially in 1968) for women to objectify men the way men have been objectifying women for centuries, but it's even more surprising to be doing it across race lines. Three white woman sing about how much they love black men, and then three black women sing about how much they love white men. The songs are funny, seemingly harmless entertainments. But there were states in the 1960s where interracial marriage was still illegal. It wasn't until *Star Trek*, in the late 60s, that television saw its first interracial kiss. These two charming songs are more subversive than the audience realizes. And though racism is far less prevalent today than it was in 1968, there are still comparatively few interracial couples in America, and, except in the biggest cities, those that exist still turn heads when they walk down the street. We haven't come as far as we'd like to think.

The drug trip makes some interesting commentary on race. When General Grant lines up his troops, not only are the genders reversed (women as Lincoln, Booth, Coolidge, Gable, etc.), but so is race in at least one case. A black woman plays Abraham Lincoln and a blond girl plays Lincoln's shoeshine boy. Like the song "Colored Spade," "Abie Baby" is another politically incorrect comedy number, in which three black tribe members sing joyously about being freed by Lincoln, in a stereotypical Hollywood black dialect. While the singers continue in the background, the black female Abe Lincoln recites a contorted Gettysburg Address, peppered with modern black references. And, as mentioned earlier, Hud becomes, just for a moment, black separatist LeRoi Jones, who threatens to kill the "interfering" white man Abraham Lincoln—still played by a black woman, of course. The joke here implies that the black separatists were so extreme they would even refuse help from the man who freed American slaves.

Interestingly, the African word *umgawa* (or *ungawa* or *Ngawa*, all interchangeable), a common rallying cry among the black empowerment movement in the 1960s, is part of the chant at the end of the show when the tribe is protesting outside the government induction center. The original Black Power chant was "beep beep, ungawa, Black Power" (with which *Hair's* original audience was no doubt familiar); in *Hair*, the hippies substitute "Flowah Powah" for "Black Power." The word *umgawa* was co-opted for a while by the *Tarzan* movies, but is now a common chant among today's young black Americans. MGM claims the word was the invention of *Tarzan* screenwriter Cyril Hume, but since there are African Americans with *Umgawa* as a last name, it's unlikely a Hollywood screenwriter thought it up. Today, the word has become very common among kids, among musicians, and in Internet chat rooms; and the Black Power chant has been co-opted and emasculated into middle school victory chants, among other things. (Try doing an Internet search for *ungawa* and see the number and variety of results, and notice how virtually none of the people using the word seem to know what it means.)

Though it's common today to practice color-blind casting— ignoring an actor's race when considering him for a role—*Hair* forced this on audiences, demanding that they think about the social roles separating the races, demanding that the audience see these separations as arbitrary and ridiculous. It's jarring to see a white girl shining shoes, but had it been a black man, we might not have even thought about it. It's odd to hear a black woman recite the Gettysburg Address, but there's no reason why she shouldn't. As she quite correctly points out, they are "*all* our forefathers." But most disturbing is that as startling as this must have been in 1968, it's still more surprising today than it should be.

Sex, Drugs, and Rock and Roll

Drugs are an important part of *Hair*—just as they were an important part of the hippie culture—and many drugs are mentioned or discussed throughout the show. The song "Hashish" lists a lot of drugs (they are discussed briefly below). In an early version of the show, this list catalogues the drugs Berger himself has ingested. In later versions, it more generally introduces the drug culture and the tribe's attitude toward drugs. The second half of the song lists prescription drugs, ironically pointing out the vast amounts of drugs ingested legally by the "older generation" while the drugs of choice of the "younger generation" are outlawed.

Hashish, a more potent grade of cannabis than marijuana, is made from resin extracted from the flower clusters and the top leaves of the marijuana plant. Hashish is usually smoked or eaten and can produce euphoria and other feelings similar to marijuana. Cocaine is found in the leaves of the South American shrub *Erythroxylon coca*. The drug induces a sense of exhilaration in the user, and it is the world's most powerful stimulant of natural origin. South American Indians have used cocaine as it occurs in the leaves of *Erythroxylon coca* for at least five thousand years. Traditionally, the leaves have been chewed for social, mystical, medicinal, and religious purposes. Opium comes from the skin of the unripe seed pods of certain poppy flowers (*Wizard of Oz*, anyone?), and farmers extract its sticky brown sap from the egg-shaped bulb. Opium's healing properties were described by Hippocrates (466–377 B.C.) and the Roman physician Galen (A.D. 130–200). The persistent role of opium as folk medicine and recreational euphoric for nearly four thousand years raises questions about the chances of its eradication any time soon.

LSD, or "acid," is the hallucinogen lysergic acid diethylamide-25. Discovered by Dr. Albert Hofmann, in 1938, LSD is one of the most potent mind-altering chemicals known. A white, odorless powder usually taken orally, its effects are highly variable and usually begin within one hour and generally last eight to twelve hours, gradually tapering off. The drug DMT was first synthesized in 1931 and was demonstrated to be hallucinogenic in 1956. It has been shown to be present in many plants. A DMT trip is very intense, with thoughts and visions coming at great speeds, producing a sense of leaving or transcending time, that objects have lost all form. When DMT is smoked or injected, effects begin in seconds, reach a peak in five to twenty minutes, and end after a half hour or so. This has earned it the name the "businessman's trip." The drug DOM, which is related to DMT, was used widely in the Haight-Ashbury neighborhood in San Francisco, in the 1960s. "Buttons" of the peyote cactus containing mescaline are dried, then chopped or ground, and sold in capsules. It is usually swallowed, but can be injected or smoked. (It was playfully nicknamed STP, after the motor oil additive, which users said stood ironically for Serenity, Tranquility, and Peace—reportedly, the stuff was horrible.)

After listing all these drugs, the lyric to the song "Hashish" deconstructs into a list of other "drugs" of mainstream society, drugs (and other addictions) of which the hippies clearly do not approve. The BMT and IRT are parts of the New York City subway system— the Brooklyn-Manhattan Transit Subway and the Interborough Rapid Transit Subway—taking thousands of people each day to their jobs. A&P was a popular grocery store chain at the time that sold alcohol and cigarettes, legal addictive drugs. Sniffing shoe polish (and other solvents and aerosols) has always been a cheap, quick, legal—but often dangerous—way to get a mild buzz. Likewise, many cough syrups contain some alcohol, so they serve as another cheap, legal way to get high.

But the real drugs here are the prescribed ones. Equinol and Thorizine are both prescription tranquilizers that were widely used by mainstream adults. Dexamyl is an amphetamine (an "upper") that was frequently prescribed as an antidepressant for bored housewives. Compazine is used primarily to prevent nausea and vomiting in cancer patients using chemotherapy, but it works just as well for trippers using hallucinogens that cause nausea. Kemadrin is used to treat and relieve the symptoms of Parkinson's disease and is also used to manage the side effects of various medicines used to treat serious mental illnesses. Kemadrin is also taken by drug users to counteract drug-induced symptoms similar to Parkinson's disease that can occur from taking Thorizine or Trilafon. Thorizine and Trilafon are narcotics often given to mental patients to calm them down. Drug users take them to calm the effects of a bad trip, and Trilafon can prevent nausea and vomiting as well. Dexedrine is an amphetamine, used today to treat Attention Deficit Disorder. Benzedrine and Methedrine, also amphetamines, were the mainstream drugs of choice for decades in America and Britain. During World War II, over seventy-two million Benzedrine pills were used by the British army. Soldiers found they could fight longer and harder when they were on the drug, and politicians and commanders took them as well. In 1946, amphetamines like Dexedrine, Benzedrine, and Methedrine were the number one prescribed medicine in America for about forty different ailments, including seasickness, migraines, impotence, weight loss, and fatigue. Over five and a half million Benzedrine pills were prescribed in 1966 alone. And one doctor prescribed an amazing twenty-four thousand ampoules of Methedrine to just a hundred patients in one year. (Interestingly, several of these drugs are spelled differently in the medical community and in the tripping community.) This sanctioned use of certain drugs while other drugs are arbitrarily condemned is further illustrated and parodied later in Act I when Berger offers "pills" (presumably legally sanctioned prescription tranquilizers) to Nixon, the Pope, and other adult authority figures.

After the song "Hashish," when Woof gets up to introduce himself, he catalogs his garden for us, flowers and foods that have spiritual and health advantages, and some that can be used as drugs. Sunflower seeds are not only a natural snack but also a mild sedative. In addition, Native Americans use them as a medicine to ease chest pain, decrease water retention, expel worms, and improve eyesight. Others say sunflower seeds can help lower blood pressure, improve cardiovascular health, suppress allergic reactions, and help people quit smoking. Some people believe sunflower essence invokes the energy of the sun, the astrological symbol of masculine energy. It strengthens male energy and the inner male, bringing about balance with the inner female (yin/yang balance). It helps resolve conflicts linked to parents and promotes a harmonious expression of one's spiritual nature. Beets are not just healthy, cleansing the blood, but they also contain the neurotransmitter and tranquilizer GABA (gamma-aminobutyric acid), a brain chemical that counteracts stress-related nerve impulses.

Woof's mention of corn is significant. Not only does corn represent for him the simpler ways of the Native Americans but also the spirituality of the ancient Mayans (whose culture was central to the hippies' philosophies). The Mayan creation story underpins the spiritual connection that many Mexicans have with corn. In their story, God molded the first people from dirt. But they couldn't pronounce the true name of the deity, so floods washed them away. When the second group of people, made of wood, committed the same sin, the creator incinerated them. Then came the third people, the people of the corn. They pronounced the true name of God and so were the chosen ones. Many people today (maybe as a result of this story) believe corn essence has a healing and spiritual use, helping to achieve a balance between heaven and earth, a grounded spirituality. Some sources say it helps "Old Souls" (those who have been here before in past lives), who find modern, urban living painful and difficult but whose wisdom and experience is needed in our society. Corn essence is said to stabilize people during spiritual expansion and help them turn these experiences into useful understanding and action. One seller of corn essence says it increases a person's ability to see value and harmony in diversity.

Sweet pea flowers are also believed to have magical powers. Some people believe that the essence of sweet pea flowers fosters a commitment to community, a social connectedness and responsibility, a sense of one's place on Earth. Others believe, even more specifically, that it corrects introverted or antisocial behavior, creates emotional stability, and helps those living in congested areas or families having trouble living together.

Morning glory seeds from the Mexican Quauhzahautl tree can be injected, producing an LSD-like experience lasting about six hours but with fewer hallucinogenic effects. Today, most commercially available morning glory seeds are treated with chemicals to render them useless as hallucinogens and to discourage their consumption. Heavenly Blue is a special variety of morning glory, the seeds of which were used by the Aztecs of Mexico to communicate with the sun gods. They would also use them as a ritual holy hallucinogen. When the Spanish came to Mexico, they tried to destroy this species of morning glory as well as many others because of their hallucinatory powers. The natives of the Oaxaca region in Mexico believe that God lives within the seeds. Moonvines are a cousin of morning glories.

Taking It All Off

In the original Broadway production, the brief nude scene at the end of Act I, during the last few bars of the song "Where Do I Go?," was optional. Each night, each actor chose whether or not to get naked. And ever since then, the nude scene has become—unintentionally—the signature moment of the show. The first question asked of anyone producing *Hair* today is, "Are you going to do the nude scene?"

But the nude scene, at least as it was originally done on Broadway, is very brief and dimly lit. And though there are opinions to the contrary, it does support and enhance the power of "Where Do I Go?" In the original production, Claude was the one member of the tribe who did not get naked. At that point in the show, he still has not decided whether to do what is "right" and live by mainstream rules or to follow Berger. But in many subsequent productions Claude has gotten naked as well, and there is a persuasive argument for his nudity. Certainly, this moment is a crossroads for Claude. His tribe is pressuring him to burn his draft card, and his parents are pressuring him to enlist in the army. But Claude just wants the freedom to live his life, to be free of the pressures of social constructs (whether of mainstream culture or counterculture), and at the end he shucks the trappings of "respectable society," the pressure to fit in, to "be an American," to go to war, and he returns to his purest form, just his bare, naked body—a rebellious act that wouldn't be considered rebellious in a more perfect world that doesn't demonize and oversexualize the human form. This act of taking his clothes off makes him vulnerable and pure and honest. And his tribe joins him in a stunning moment of support and communalism. With or without Claude's participation, it is an important moment, free of sexuality and (thanks to the dim lights) relatively free of voyeurism. It really is about freedom in its purest form, and appropriately, *freedom* is the last word the tribe sings as the song ends.

Yes, the show can work without the nude scene, but it then loses some of its power, because its absence dilutes the notions of rule busting and the rejection of the mindlessly conforming values of mainstream society. And yes, some productions move the nudity to other moments like the trip or "The Bed" (which sexualizes the nudity inappropriately). But as with almost everything in *Hair*, the original moment works best. And happily, once audiences see the nude scene in context, it loses its most of its "naughtiness," and the drama and power of Claude's existential questions take center stage.

7/   Let the Sun Shine In

S ince my involvement with *Hair* began, in 2000, I have met so many people who have been changed by the show. Bradley Calise, of our Osage Tribe in St. Louis, says, "*Hair* was the first show I have ever done where I really felt as though I was saying something important, and, perhaps even more important, it was the first show I have done where I really believed in what I was saying. Though the show is over thirty years old, any criticisms about its being dated have never held much weight with me. While the main conflict (Vietnam) is no longer being fought, the scars of that war live on to this day, just as many of the other issues in the show do (racism, acceptance of those different from you, the ridiculous and arbitrary way society stigmatizes all recreational drugs). As I became more and more involved in *Hair*, everything we were fighting for in the show became more important to me, and I began to understand how it must have felt when people began reaching out to one another in the sixties, with the hopes that they would actually make the world a better place."

Mo Monahan, also of our Osage Tribe, says, "As with every family in the 1960s, our lives were changed by the Vietnam War. What was once a typical family of kids, high school, school plays, and sports had turned into a life of impending doom. My two older brothers were drafted into the army. Our home was filled with quiet fear of the dreaded phone call that they were 'going over.' No one really talked about it until their friends who were there sent letters. Here I was a little girl listening to stories of shrapnel imbedded in the arms, legs, and faces of the boys I'd known all my life. I tried to escape from the nightmare of what was happening around me. But how could I? Dan Rather, war correspondent, was showing me images every night on the news of bloody bodies, stories of torture, POWs, and the horrors of 'the real world.' I felt utterly confused, helpless, and totally freaked out that my brothers might be included in the body count of the dead. Children should not believe that war is a part of life. I thought every generation *had* to have a war. After all, my grandfather was in World War I and my dad in World War II. Doing *Hair* helped me break out and shout to the world to stop the violence, stop the prejudice. *Hair* gave me the hope of peace and the realization that I can make a difference. I could finally speak out and express the emotions that I had kept inside me, so tormented, at the age of twelve. I am a new person because of *Hair*. If we speak out about the injustices of the world, someone will listen. The audience listened and I felt empowered and it has overflowed into my life and I will never be the same."

Beck Hunter, another Osage Tribe member, says, "I could scarcely contain my surprise when *Hair* really came together in a big way. Not only were our audiences totally digging our performances, but as a group our tribe was bonding in a way that no one expected. The idea that doing *Hair* will change your life was really true. I cried myself nearly to sickness and shrieked myself hoarse each night because the show and the pain of experiencing that life had become so real to me. I wasn't just playing Jeanie, I *was* her, and these were my dear friends who were being sent to fight a war, many never to return. And while I often can't verbalize the power this show has on those of us who are lucky enough to bring it to life, I choose to think of our tribe as messengers. Messengers who had only one month to share our knowledge with as many people as we could."

Mike Heeter, the Osage Tribe's Claude (in the second production), tells an amazing story:

> "Can I have your headband?" It seemed like an innocent enough request from the sweet, smiling, grandma type standing in front of

me after our final *Hair* performance, September 1, 2001. Following nearly every show, the scene was similar—people pouring out of their seats to fill the stage floor, dancing with the cast, hugging, crying, and telling their own stories of the Johnson/Nixon Era. But this woman's agenda was different. She tapped me on the shoulder, turned me around to face her and grabbed my hands. She just stared at me with wet eyes for what was beginning to be an uncomfortable amount of time. She said nothing. She followed it up with a surprisingly strong hug and finally the question—"Can I have your headband?"

Playing Claude in our production, I found that people had strange reactions to me after the show. Having just seen Claude murdered in the jungles of Vietnam only to appear once more as a ghostly vision, some people were hesitant to talk to me. Some wouldn't even make eye contact. But there were others still who only wanted to tell me about their personal Vietnam experiences—the political atmosphere in the late sixties and early seventies, the horrible memories of the draft, and the young people they lost to Vietnam.

But this woman wanted my headband—a simple, red, western-patterned handkerchief that I had folded to tie around my head. It was used to reflect the fashion of the period, but mostly I tied it on to hold my wig tightly in place. 'I would love for you to have it,' I said, and walked with her on my arm to the backstage area. Along the way, she told me how much she enjoyed the show, how it made her feel, and about the nineteen-year-old son she lost to Vietnam. As she took the headband from me, she again grabbed my hands and said, "My son used to wear a headband just like this and I wanted to keep it to help me remember."

My mind went numb. Nothing I could've said would have made a difference anyway. It just sent a breaker of emotion that started at the base of my neck, up and over my head like a hood. I had no use for the headband any longer. The show was over and it was time to move on. I just thanked the woman for coming to the show, hugged her, and zombied upstairs to the dressing rooms. As I stripped out of my character's final soldier's dress uniform and began putting on my real-world clothes of jeans, tennis shoes, and a T-shirt, it smacked me hard. The idea that *Hair* wasn't just some relic of sixties Flower Power. Its effects have reached way beyond that. This show that seems so dated on the exterior is still having a profound effect on every member of its audience and anyone involved in its production. This woman's simple request broke through my opaque walls, and the sun came piercing through. Taking stock, reprioritizing, and connecting with people in ways I had long forgotten—it's all in my future now. I'm following the river in my heart. Down to the gutter. Up to the glitter. Into the city where the truth lies.

In a continuing two-man back-and-forth, John Sparger, the man who first played Berger under my direction, and I have plumbed *Hair's* depths many times. He was brilliant in the role, electrifying. He and I bonded over this show in a profound way that will probably last both our lives. The following is one of the more recent things he wrote to me about *Hair*:

They say it's a dead show. A dated show. They (read: critics) say there's no point in performing the show these days. People are no longer interested in the Hare Krishna of flower children tripping out of a counterculture long gone.

I couldn't disagree more.

Despite its seemingly quasi-loose structure, authority-bashing irreverence, and Vietnam-era backdrop, *Hair's* message is as necessary in the present as it was in the late sixties. Make love, not war; peace on Earth and good will to all creatures; do unto others. . . . True, there are numerous productions of *Hair* being spewed forth as so much excrement on stages from Poughkeepsie to Pomona. But when care is given to depth, enlightenment will emerge.

Hair was always one of those shows on my To Do list—with Berger being the prize role. What more could a long-haired, rock n' rollin' hippie wannabe want out of theatre? I thought my life at the time (sex, drugs, struggling artist) was perfect for the essence of the character. Yet, for all those years I jonesed for my shot, an opportunity never presented itself. Ironically, it was some time later, during one of my "cleansing periods" that I was cast. And it was the absence of the aforementioned intoxicants that enabled me greater insight into this character and this show.

Although sex and drugs in their many variations play a part in *Hair,* I feel they are merely accelerants toward the larger meaning—peace, love, and understanding, acceptance, brotherhood. So instead of smoking pot, dropping acid, and engaging in a sampling of sexual scenarios, I confronted the show's content with a clear head and a clean shell. Expansion of the mind attained from the heart and soul can be longer lasting and more rewarding. At least it was for me.

Hair is a show in which the whole is certainly nothing without its parts, but also where the parts are nothing unto themselves till summed. Yes, we all know "Aquarius" and the title song "Hair." And most of us recognize "Easy to Be Hard." But the book itself is a series of mostly nonlinear non sequiturs strung out in a drug-induced mélange, thinly plotted against the political and cultural climate of the times. Or is it?

Here we have a cat—Claude, who owns up to his civic duty—scratch, make that moral duty as a sacrifice of physical being for the betterment of . . . hell, I'm not sure even he knows what he's dying for. But there must be some justice in it, right? 'Cause he knows he ain't coming back.

Now, whether Berger understands the politics behind the war—scratch, make that conflict—or he's just not into laying his life down for ol' Uncle Sam, he's definitely not interested in being a cog in a machine that kills rather than loves. And he certainly can't understand why his best friend feels the need to mount the cross.

Each is attacking the enemy from a different front. But exactly who is the enemy?

The beauty of this show is within the couching of its agenda. For underneath it all, *Hair* is a morality play. The tribe in a fight against the authority of the times with its savior (Claude) caught in a struggle to sacrifice the flesh to save the soul.

Breaking the staid and stagnant conventions of the 1950s allows the participants of this new generation to unshackle themselves and elevate to a higher plane. Certain drugs and sexual freedoms are ways of opening up to greater possibilities. But the strongest tool available is, of course, the mind. For when the mind is free, there are no limits.

Michael Butler, who produced the original Broadway production of *Hair*, has talked to me at great length about how the *Hair* tribes around the world can come together and make a difference in the world. He wrote this to me in the summer of 2002:

The sixties were a period of great hope. Even after the shock of Jack Kennedy's assassination, his mantra of the future continued to stimulate youth—those young in spirit besides those young in body. Those of the movement felt we had a real chance to bring peace and love to the world. Freedom was the passion. Spirituality was the driving power. Compassion was a rule and the environment a concern. Many were in states of altered consciousness arrived at through various disciplines, including, for the impatient, mind-elevating substances.

Toward the end of the sixties hope was changing to fear. Many felt that we in the United States were heading for another civil war. *Hair* arrived at this time to be a beacon of hope through a dialogue between the generations. The proscenium arch was broken to bring the audience into the tribe. *Hair* explained many of the problems facing the world as seen by the young. We were attacked by both the radical left and the radical right.

The murder of Martin Luther King, then Robert Kennedy, the riots at Columbia University, began to change fear to rage. An example was the actions of the yuppies who set up Mayor Daley at the Democratic Convention in Chicago. We warned the mayor this was going to happen. He could not believe that the violence was a planned event. The paranoid reaction of the authorities is what gave us Richard Nixon as president. Force on all sides began to strip the power of our spiritual quest. Then we had Kent State.

Realization began to set in that those of the movement could not prevail against the establishment. We did not know how to run or to be within the system. Many began to drop out. A new mantra—instead of "om," the saying became "getting our shit together." Materialism became paramount. A job was the rule, working for the establishment, pursuing such dreams as a white-picketed yard surrounding a suburban house. Extremism is so the rule in this country. The next step was "greed is good." Ushered in was a period of the pursuit of wealth that made the times of the robber barons seem benign.

Free trade, a drive against world poverty, has been corrupted by globalization. Organized religions are increasingly influenced by fundamentalism. The planet is damaged by insensitive use of our natural resources. The gap between the poor and the rich gets larger. The world is awash with corrupt governments. In this country we are ruled by a regime whose election remains questioned. Americans are faced with a spiritual crisis—a bereavement of spirit.

So much seems wrong, one crisis after another. We have been struck by a vicious act of terror. We do not understand where such hatred comes from. Our isolation and unilateral government gives rise to the perception that we don't care about the problems of the world. Our supposed economic miracle is coming unglued. Corporate misadventures and executive greed have plundered the savings of many. Our own indulgence in the economic bubble has brought about serious financial problems. We lack leadership and statesmanship that allow us to feel confident about the future.

There is a strong feeling, or at least a hope, that something or someone will appear to lead us out of the wilderness. Meanwhile the best solution is that we have to lead ourselves. Each person needs to do what he or she can to help the problems of the community, the nation, and the world. We are all one. Everyone can do something to improve our planet physically, mentally, and spiritually, to at least reduce the mess we are leaving the young.

The tribes of *Hair* can do quite a bit toward these endeavors. Individually, collectively, and through the show, we are in a unique position to carry such messages. So many people over the world have seen *Hair*, more than any other musical, and they remember it well. *Hair* continues to be performed in many colleges and high schools. Young people want to know the truth about the sixties and their forebears want to relive those days. Those who have experienced altered forms of consciousness, by whatever means, never forget that space in which they have been. Now they have learned how to function within the system. It is time they act to run it.

# Resources

A version of the script that lies somewhere between the off Broadway and Broadway versions was published but is currently out of print. You may be able to find it in used-bookstores or on the web (there are often copies on Ebay). Also out of print but worth finding are two books about the show, Barbara Lee Horn's *The Age of Hair: Evolution and Impact of Broadway's First Rock Musical,* and Lorrie Davis and Rachel Gallagher's *Letting Down My Hair.* Davis was an original Broadway cast member, and her book describes the creation of the show, although it has been accused of major inaccuracies. Almost every newspaper article about the original productions can be found on the web at *www.michaelbutler.com/hairpages.* Vocal selections are commercially available, but the full score and the Broadway script are available only through Tams-Witmark, which licenses performances.

There are many recordings of the score available on CD. The best is the original Broadway cast album, but the 1993 London revival cast album contains new music that has now been incorporated into the standard rental version. The original off Broadway cast album (which is very different) and a recording of songs cut from the show called *DisinHAIRited* are both only on out-of-print LPs, but both are worth finding. There is also the invaluable *Hair* Online

Archives (at *www.michaelbutler.com/hair/*) as well as an active and invaluable e-mail discussion list about *Hair* on the Internet that can be accessed at *www.jabberwocky.com*. This discussion list counts among its members dozens of actors, directors, and designers who have worked on *Hair*, as well as members of the original Broadway cast. Past posts are archived on the website. Members of the list helped me immeasurably in researching *Hair* both for my own productions and for this book. A new, *official Hair* website can be found at *www.hairthemusical.com*.

The full text of Allen Ginsberg's poem "Wichita Vortex Sutra," on which the song "Three-Five-Zero-Zero" is based, can be found in *Allen Ginsberg: Selected Poems 1947–1995*, published by HarperCollins.

Also interesting is the documentary *Grass*, a fascinating and highly entertaining history of marijuana use and governmental repression during the twentieth century. Other films that help explain the sixties are *Easy Rider* and *Woodstock*.

So Now What?

I t's not enough that we talk about the issues in *Hair*. It's not enough that we feel bad about the fact that all these years later we haven't yet solved any of the problems *Hair* dramatizes. It's not enough that we think about all these issues now and then. Where does that thinking take us when we walk out of the theatre or we hear the last strains of "Let the Sun Shine In" and turn off the CD player?

Below is a list of organizations you can contact and/or join and do something about making the world a better place. We *can* right the wrongs *Hair* brings to light. We can get involved in those causes, we can contribute to them, we can call and write, we can volunteer our time. We can make a difference.

Don't let this be the last time you think about the issues in *Hair*, about what's wrong with our world. Do something about it. Do what *Hair* asks of us—let the sun shine in, before it's too late.

Amnesty International
322 8th Avenue
New York, NY 10001
(212) 807-8400
www.amnesty.org

NAACP
4805 Mt. Hope Drive
Baltimore, MD 21215
(410) 521-4939
www.naacp.org

MTV's Fight for Your Rights: Take a Stand Against Discrimination
www.fightforyourrights.mtv.com

Doctors Without Borders
6 E. 39th St., 8th floor
New York, NY 10016
(212) 679-6800
www.dwb.org or *www.doctorswithoutborders.org*

Heifer Project International
P.O. Box 8058
Little Rock, AR 72203
(800) 422-0474
www.heifer.org

Nature Conservancy
4245 North Fairfax Drive, Suite 100
Arlington, VA 22203-1606
(800) 628-6860
www.nature.org

Earth Island Institute
300 Broadway, Suite 28
San Francisco, CA 94133-3312
(415) 788-3666
www.earthisland.org

National Organization for the Reformation of Marijuana Laws
(NORML)
1001 Connecticut Ave. NW, Suite 710
Washington, DC 20036
(202) 483-5500
www.norml.org

Protest.Net
Worldwide calendar offers locations, dates, and information for activism, protests, pickets, strikes, demonstrations, meetings, and direct political action.
www.protest.net

Electronic Activist
E-mail address directory of U.S. representatives and senators, state governments, and media entities. Also includes activism how-to.
www.berkshire.net/~ifas/activist/

Progressive Secretary
Letter-writing cooperative that sends out e-mails to Congress, the President, and elected officials on peace, ecology, civil rights, and other issues. Topics and messages are suggested and selected by participants.
www.progressivesecretary.org

E-The People
A nonpartisan site working with over four hundred online newspapers, television stations, and Internet portals to bring government closer to the people, allowing users to send an e-mailed or faxed letter or a petition to over thousands of federal, state, and local officials.
www.ethepeople.com